Expressing Theology

Expressing Theology

A Guide to Writing Theology that Readers Want to Read

Jonathan C. Roach
Gricel Dominguez

CASCADE *Books* · Eugene, Oregon

EXPRESSING THEOLOGY
A Guide to Writing Theology that Readers Want to Read

Cascade Books
An Imprint of Wipf and Stock Publishers
199 W. 8th Ave., Suite 3
Eugene, OR 97401

www.wipfandstock.com

ISBN 13: 978-1-4982-0870-3

Cataloging-in-Publication data:

Roach, Jonathan C.

    Expressing theology : a guide to writing theology that readers want to read / Jonathan C. Roach and Gricel Dominguez.

    xiv + 168 p. ; 23 cm. —Includes bibliographical references and index(es).

    ISBN 13: 978-1-4982-0870-3

    1. Writing. 2. Theology—Methodology. 3. Authorship—Religious aspects—Christianity. 4. Authorship—Handbooks, manuals, etc. I. Dominguez, Gricel. II. Title.

PN147 E9 2015

Manufactured in the U.S.A.

Dedication

Jonathan dedicates this book to his wife, Jihey Esther Roach, and their daughter, Enye Grace Roach.

Gricel dedicates this book to her mother and grandfather, neither of whom understood what all the writing was about, but who supported her all the same.

Table of Contents

Foreword

Let's face it; most theology is boring. Few see the real importance of a theological work, and most of us can't name a theologian, let alone see a reason to become one. One reason for this may be that theology, in the past few decades, has been written more and more by academics for academics, and less and less for the average Christian or the broader world. Jonathan and Gricel are looking to start a revolution. They want to overthrow this whole dynamic. They want to buck the trend of boring theology and help move talk about God back to the heart of everyday life. And this book is the catalyst to get that revolution started.

Expressing Theology will help you to write engaged, compelling, and beautiful theology. For starters, it will help you to look at yourself as a theologian and a writer. Whether you are a student, early in your writing career, or an established theologian, coming to terms with your identity as a theologian and a writer is a difficult but essential process. It is essential because theology and writing are both inherently self-involving processes. There is no way to write theology without getting to the core of who you are and how you see the world. There is no way to write theology without staring down your demons and pouring yourself into your words. As Jonathan and Gricel point out, you can hide yourself behind a barrage of technical terms and a maelstrom of passive sentences, but you can't get away from involving your deepest self in the process.

Maybe that is why *Expressing Theology* is such a revolution. It asks you to put yourself into your theological writing. Not only by sharing your most fundamental convictions about the world and how it works, but by sharing them in your own voice. Sure you will find tons of ideas here about the writing process—really practical, down to earth stuff like where and when to write and what you should have in your hand while you are writing. But, what makes this book a real revolution is that it asks you to be yourself in a really public way. That's scary.

The best theology has always been self-implicating. Just read one of St. Paul's letters and you will hear his personality jumping off the page. (Remember this one?: "You foolish Galatians! Who has bewitched you?"). The same is true for Augustine, Anselm, Bernard, and dozens of others. With the really great theologians, you feel like you know them through their words. That is probably because you do. And sharing yourself with your audience is exactly what makes writing theology so scary.

The practice of writing in fear starts for lots of us in school; at least it did for me. Maybe you are afraid that you won't get the grade that you want. Or maybe you are afraid that you aren't as smart as the rest of the class. Maybe you are afraid that you won't be any good at the things that are most important to you. Graduate school, professional writing and doctoral dissertations only increase the stakes. But isn't it time we stopped all that nonsense?

Jonathan and Gricel have read a lot of bad theology and are dedicated to helping improve it. They have worked with countless students over the years, helping them to organize their thoughts, research topics, develop drafts, and revise rough documents. They also are practicing the craft of writing themselves. Both of them have struggled to find their own voice in writing and have struggled, in quiet rooms by themselves and in writing communities, to develop their craft. They realize that learning to write is a journey and that it develops over time. *Expressing Theology* shares the fruit of what they have learned along this journey and helps its readers move forward on the path to theological writing that is exciting.

I am proud to be invited to introduce this book to you. It was a joy to read for me and I have better tools as a writer because of it. It has helped me to think about the process of writing theology. After reading it, I am more aware of my good and bad habits as a writer and a theologian. I am also better equipped to break the bad habits and reinforce the positive ones. Recognizing your strengths as a writer can also help make the writing process more fun.

I believe that *Expressing Theology* can help lots of you to become better writers and theologians too. It can help you to find your own voice, improve as a writer and as a theologian, and maybe even learn to enjoy the writing process. It might even help you to be more comfortable with who you really are and what you really think. That is a revolution I am excited to see.

Theodore James Whapham
Dean, School of Ministry
University of Dallas

Acknowledgments

It takes a community to raise a book, and I want to take a few lines to thank the community that raised this book. I want to thank my family for their support during the writing process: Rev. Jihey Esther Roach, my wife, L. Kay Roach, my mother, and Rev. Chan A. Roach, my father. Without their support I couldn't have finished. I also thank the faculty and staff of the University Library at St. Thomas University: Susan Angulo, Jonathan Best, Isabel Ezquerra, Gretel la Guardia, Isabel Medina, Nina Rose, Cindy Stafford, Larry Treadwell, and Elliot Williams. Next, I want to thank the many sudents, doctoral canadiates, and fellow theologians who gave the feedback that shaped this book: Claudia Herrera, Jonathan Best, Pat Doody, Ted Whapham, and Emmanuel Buteau, as well as the students in the 2014 Winter Semester course on Theogloical Writing and Research at St. Thomas University for their helpful insights. I also want to thank the wonderful women and men who have taught me theology: Anneliese Sinnott OP, Mary Carter Waren, Pat Benson OP, David Cleaver- Bartholomew, Urias Beverly, V. Bruce Rigdon, Tony Curtis Henderson, Oscar King III, Kenneth Harris, Olaf Lidums, James Perkinson, Charles Packer, Bryan Froehle, and Bernard Lee SM. Next, I want to thank two fanistic Graduate Assistants Jules Wigel and Liedy Quintal for their help in the research process. Finally, I couldn't have finished this project without my co-author Gricel Dominguez who has a magical touch for shaping narravitve.

Thank you.

Jonathan

I would like to thank Jonathan for taking a chance on a writer with no theological background and too many opinions on grammar. I would also like to thank my mom for the little things that made it possible for me to focus on writing, my special someone for keeping me grounded when I needed a reality check, and those who put up with my rants on bad writing.

Thank you.

Gricel

one

Writing Theology

I'm sparking a revolution. Want to join me? I'll warn you—the pay's terrible (zero actually) and there's a high chance of failure. The status quo fights dirty. We'll be swimming against the tide . . . but the prize will be all the sweeter for it.

If anyone ever told me I would become a rebel, I would've called them crazy. Growing up in small-town Middle America during the eighties, I didn't like change. I benefited from the status quo. Let's put it out there . . . I'm a WASP; a white, Anglo-Saxon, Protestant male with all the privileges and power that entails, whether I choose to recognize it or not. I was comfortable with myself and the world I lived in. After all, I was on top. All that changed in 2012. After writing a dissertation on practical theology to earn my PhD, I became passionate about transforming how we write theology. I want a revolution. I demand change. Readers deserve better!

I want to spark a revolution that transforms how theologians from all walks of life and traditions express theology. I believe theology should be engaging, compelling, and beautiful. No matter the audience we're trying to reach, the language, the engagement with Scripture, the exploration of human experience should resonate in the mind and soul of the reader. Whether the reader loves our content or hates it, theology should be a joy to read.

"Bad" Theology

Reading "bad" theology hurts. The reasons for this pain are numerous, but there are three major symptoms: poor writing skills, shallow writing, and

1

fear. These three make painkillers useless against the torment of reading bad theology. Poor writing skills include incorrect grammar, confusing sentence construction, and common usage and punctuation mistakes, but the biggest culprit behind poor writing remains lousy style: wordy, fat sentences that are held together by weak verbs; choppy, repetitive sentence construction; unclear, boring prose that commits to nothing; and writing that lacks personality and fails to draw the reader in through examples such as stories and illustrations exemplify lousy style. If the prose could've been written by a robot, it lacks style. Think of the "voice" that your GPS or smartphone uses to communicate—monotone, no inflection, emotion, or even an accent to distinguish it. This lack of style happens when writers try to sound "academic." In trying to sound academic, writers lose their personality and voice in an attempt to sound like everyone else, even if everyone else is doing a bad job of writing.

The second major factor behind bad theology is *shallow* writing. Teachers know shallow writing when they read it. It happens when writers aren't prepared to write. Shallow writers spew words on the page without purpose or direction. Students call this "BS" writing, which means that the words don't actually accomplish anything other than fill up pages. Shallow writers dash off whatever pops into their heads without integration or reflection. They write about personal experiences, but never explain what these experiences mean. I often find myself wondering if shallow writers think their readers are psychic because only a mind-reader could connect the dots and find meaning in their seemingly random comments.

Another common symptom of shallow writing happens when writers spend two or three paragraphs summarizing a source, and then begin summarizing another source, on and on without reflecting or discussing the material or trying to bring it together. I can even visualize them writing. They grab one book or article, scan it quickly, pull one or two ideas or quotes to write about, then pick up another source and do it again. They continue this pattern until reaching the minimum number of pages required by their professor. Then, they stop writing—no conclusion, no summary, no reflection. They just stop. It's shallow, superficial writing that gives readers nothing new or original. Shallow writing just takes up space. Reading it feels meaningless.

The fear-based writer is related to the shallow writer. Fear-based writers believe they have nothing worth adding to the conversation. They fear that their readers will think they are stupid or ignorant if they write their own ideas, insights, and stories. They add dense, long, verbatim quotes to their papers, perhaps adding a sentence or two of their own in between. The worst fear-based writers of theology just list Scripture citation after Scripture citation because what can be a greater source than the Bible? In their minds, no one can argue with the Bible and clearly there is only one interpretation of the Bible. By using these long quotes from the "experts" and from Scripture, fear-based writers hide themselves and their ideas behind the words of others to avoid being exposed. They worry about what their readers will think of them. They believe published theologians must be brilliant, so there is nothing they can add to the discourse that can make it any better . . . they often fear they'll make it worse. They're afraid they will misinterpret a great concept and readers will think they are stupid, or they fear having their insights stand along those of published authors, and then being read and misunderstood themselves because they couldn't express their ideas effectively. These writers allow fear to control them and the results are terrible to read.

"Bad" theology is not just a problem for student writers. Poorly written theology littered with lousy style, shallow prose, and fear-based writing appears in published books all the time. Sometimes the bad writing habits that students pick up in high school and college continue to haunt their dissertations and published works. As a PhD candidate, I became so frustrated after reading piles of theological books filled with brilliant theological insights buried beneath poorly written prose that I decided to start this revolution. It's time for readers to enjoy reading theology.

TAKE A MOMENT TO REFLECT

1. What was your worst experience reading theology? What made it so bad?

2. Have you ever been afraid to voice your thoughts? To share your writing?

Words, Words, Words

For human beings, words exist as an inexhaustible source of wonder, insight, and understanding. Words are as capable of inflicting great injury as they are of bringing healing and love to ease the deepest wounds and pains. Whether shared over dinner or printed in books, words represent our most basic way of communicating our experience of the world around us. Wordsmiths craft words into powerful representations of the human experience that transcend centuries, capturing the greatest and the worst of what it means to be human. For generations, poets, actors, playwrights, preachers, novelists, songwriters, and theologians have crafted words into verses and sentences profound with meaning. Words make people stop and think; words propel people to action; words provoke deep emotional responses; words bring comfort; and words start wars.

Words have been used to justify slavery and genocide. Theologians built a theology upon the Curse of Ham[1] that not only justified slavery but argued that the enslavement of human beings from Africa was mandated by the Bible. Politicians shape words into propaganda, or the more friendly sounding concept of "controlling the narrative," to sell their agendas or themselves. With a few simple words and powerful images, advertisers create new markets. Marketers convince people to buy a product or lead a lifestyle, even when consumers can't afford it or it might harm their health and wellbeing. Writing theology comes with a tremendous responsibility to yourself, to your readers, and to God. Words can do great harm to people's lives, emotions, and spirits. Careless, and sometimes unintentional, words *do* harm.

But words also have the potential to do incredible good. One Sunday, after a sermon when I quoted the children's song *Jesus Loves Me*, an older woman explained to me that the words of that song saved her childhood. She told me that she first heard that song as a small child growing up in Northern Michigan at a local Methodist church. Hearing that song was the first time that she heard someone loved her. Those simple words formed the whole foundation of her spirituality and gave her enough spiritual power to thrive in light of the abusive environment that surrounded her early life. Words woven into narratives, lyrics, and stories create spaces for reconciliation, social justice, and lasting peace. In 1962, Rachel Carson wrote *Silent Spring*, which started the contemporary environmental movement in the United States. Think of the words of Martin Luther King Jr., of Malcolm X, or of Winston Churchill. The right words create amazing change in the hands and minds of readers. They light fires, bring down corruption, foster

1. Genesis 9:21–27.

hope, and save lives. Words can and do great good. They can bring wellness, healing, and hope on the darkest nights of the soul.

I find it helpful to engage a farming metaphor. Imagine growing words as crops. Imagine a garden of words overflowing with colors and flavors. The agriculture metaphor of farming captures two very important aspects of writing. First, words, like plants, need to grow. A single word is like a seed, full of potential and possibility. Words need to be planted in the deep soil of human experience so they can send down roots that touch the basic needs of humanity, and bring forth shoots and stems that reach up for the dreams and visions of a better future. But, like a farmer, the writer cannot just drop a seed into soil and walk away. Words must be carefully nourished. They need to be pruned and shaped. Unnecessary words need to be weeded away. And like the farmer, the theologian needs to provide the right amounts of water, sunlight, and nutrients during the proper season of the year for the seed to grow into award-winning, beautiful narratives.

Secondly, these farmed words need to foster hope in the light of feeding readers. We need to grow words with a purpose. Farming reflects the purpose writers of theology need to cultivate in their work. Farming isn't about growing rows of corn and acres of potatoes and letting the crops rot in the field. We need to do something with the crops. We need to plant words with a purpose to feed the spiritually hungry, to bring people together around a table of fellowship, to nourish.

Theology comes in many forms and mediums as varied as the human imagination. There are no ends to the ways in which you can express theology. From the most ancient cave paintings and carvings, to music and soaring architecture, theology remains a human meditation on the divine. Sometimes theology becomes a quest and sometimes it encapsulates silence. Theologians live common, everyday lives, sometimes at the margins of life, helping fellow pilgrims come closer to God and each other. The only thing that limits theology is the human imagination. Theology can be found in beauty, and theology can be found in the twisted and ugly. While my work here concerns written theology, I celebrate that written theology remains only one small slice of the theological pie. Music, dance, painting, just to name a few, provide wonderful and very important examples of theological expression beyond the scope of my work in this book. Wherever and whenever people of faith express their questions, hopes, and concerns to God and others, this is theology.

What's Theology?

Saint Anselm provides one of the most fundamental and important definitions of theology: "faith seeking understanding."[2] This remains the classical definition of theology. This doesn't mean that faith seeks to replace understanding; rather, faith seeking understanding reflects an active process where human faith attempts to grow into a deeper understanding of the divine. Anselm lived during the eleventh century and entered an abbey in Normandy as a novice in 1060 CE. By 1093 CE, he became the Archbishop of Canterbury. Throughout his career Anselm wrote theology. Theologians have been rewriting and building upon Anselm's definition for centuries, as South African theologian James Cochrane does when he writes "theology is reflection on faith in the world in order to make sense of reality."[3] Theology is faith asking questions and looking for answers. This captures the heart of faith seeking understanding.

Theology embraces everything associated with the church, faith, Scripture, life, ministry, the divine, spirituality, and the interpretation of the relationships between any of these concepts and God. This includes everything and anything from economics to the latest video game. The word theology comes from two Greek words: *Theos*—meaning the divine and/or God—and *logia*—sayings, accounts, teachings, and theories.[4] *Theos* + *logia* = theology. The ultimate concern that separates theology from religious studies remains theology's God-centeredness. Without God and God's message to the world, words are not theology.

Dorotheus of Gaza, a sixth-century Syrian monk, gives the best illustration for my understanding of theology. Dorotheus writes,

2. Williams, "Saint Anselm."
3. Cochrane, *Circles of Dignity*, 153.
4. Stone and Duke, *How to Think Theologically*, 7.

Imagine a circle marked out on the ground. Suppose that this circle is the world and that the center of the circle is God. Leading from the edge to the center are a number of lines, representing ways of life. In their desire to draw near to God, the saints advance along these lines to the middle of the circle, so that the further they go, the nearer they approach to one another as well as to God. The closer they come to God, the closer they come to one another. . . . Such is the nature of love; the nearer we draw to God in love, the more we are united together by the love for our neighbor.[5]

This theological model brings people into closer relationship with their Creator and their fellow humans in this world. Building on Dorotheus's illustration, I define theology as a spirit-embodied dialogical process for community-discerned sustainable action. Transformation characterizes this model of theology. Theology exists as a God-filled process from beginning to end that engages in dialogue with self and others, Scripture and tradition, other disciplines, insiders and outsiders, and the communities of faith. This discernment requires a communal spiritual process that includes worship, prayer, and active spiritual listening to God and others, and a group approach to interpretation that fosters sustainable action. This group discernment makes room for listening for the insights inspired by God, and for being inspired by God through the voices of each person in the encounter. I will explore the concept of group theological interpretation and discernment in more detail in chapter 3.

My definition of theology relies upon understanding the relationship between theology and spirituality. I believe theology cannot and should not be separated from spirituality. Theologian Thomas Groome reminds us the separation between theology and spirituality that emerged in scholastic theology "enfeebled" both disciplines.[6] I contend all theologians must engage theology and spirituality as two sides of the same coin. Theology demands both to be an authentic expression of either discipline. Theology, which bridges the division between theology and spirituality, empowers holistic theological approaches to address separation of mind, body, and spirit.

Another split also hurts theology, this time between practice and theory. This split causes damage both to theology and to the practice of faith. Abstract theoretical theology often presents a maze of ideas that lead

5. Dorotheus of Gaza, *Discourses and Sayings,* 138–39.

6. Groome, *Sharing Faith,* 55.

nowhere. Theology must be rooted in the experience of life and the practices of faith. Theology must connect life—work, food, housing, transportation, money, family, friends—with the practices of faith—prayer, congregational life, pastoral care, preaching, religious formation. A Christology that does not embody the incarnation of Jesus into the realities of life fails. It might be fully divine, but it is not fully human. Vague, abstract concepts will float up to heaven but their feet will lose all contact with the earth. Theology must relate to lived experiences both in everyday practices and the practices of faith, which for some people might be exclusive and for others, deeply intertwined if not one and the same.

Theology must also transform. Transforming practice includes the encounter with alterity, as theologian Elaine Graham names the concept.[7] This is another way of saying that transforming practice must include experiencing different ways of being or doing. I find Graham's benchmarks of transformation important as part of my theological process to overcome the splits between theology and spirituality as well as practices and theory. These benchmarks include offering revealing encounters with alterity, "excavating and evaluating the sources or norms for practice," "providing dignity and equality" to people as their faith is "renewed by mutuality and self-acceptance," moving "beyond," which is only possible if the person "is forever grounded, in the immediate," and causing a shift "from ontology to practice" (i.e., orthopraxis).[8] These benchmarks translate into approaches that allow theologians to open themselves to the divine, to critically examine what has happened, to discover dignity and equality as they are renewed in their communities of faith and in their own self-acceptance, and finally to shift from thinking about orthodoxy to living orthopraxis. Orthodoxy in this use doesn't mean the branches of the church like Greek Orthodox or Russian Orthodox; rather, orthodoxy means right thinking while orthopraxis means doing something the right way. Therefore, transformation in theology requires people to change from thinking about doing the right thing to actually doing the right thing.

7. Alterity, according to theologian Elaine Graham "is one way of regarding human identity, meaning and community as both singular and interdependent, and reflects the necessity and contingency of 'otherness.' Alterity expresses the paradox at the heart of the human experience, that identity is founded on solipsism and individualism, of experiencing the Other as completely alien and inaccessible, but that the boundaries of identity are dependent upon the existence and particularity of others." Graham, *Transforming Practice*, 168.

8. Ibid., 204–7.

Writing transformational theology that reads as engaging, compelling, and beautiful prose is a difficult endeavor. It is hard to write good theology. Thomas Merton, one of the greatest theologians of the twentieth century, writes, "it is extremely difficult to write theology well. The main reason I can't write it is that I don't know it. I don't know precisely what I want to say, and therefore when I start to write I find that I am working out a theology as I go."[9] Wow! If Thomas Merton finds it hard, how hard will it be for the rest of us? I never said that this revolution was going to be easy. Writing good theological prose is never easy. But Merton has given theologians a key place to start with this statement. Writing theology becomes very difficult if you are writing by the seat of your pants. If you make it up as you go, chances are you will wander all over the place before going nowhere. And while you are wandering in the desert of content, it becomes easy to forget the value of a good writing style. When you combine content that goes nowhere with poorly written prose, you have a recipe for bad theology.

One key factor in writing theology that blooms with theological growth and well-being is to write theology rather than just writing *about* theology. This can be a very fine detail, but it is a critical concept. Writing that only summarizes other theologies, or traces the history of a theological concept, may not be theology unless it bridges the historical interpretation and the modern world in order to draw people closer to God and each other. I value the important role historical theology plays as it explores how a theological concept has been shaped and interpreted throughout the Christian tradition, but historic theology must take the next critical step of engaging the historical with today's reality. It starts with the writer's purpose. Are you writing knowledge for the sake of knowledge? Or does your writing attempt to bring people into an experience of the divine? Defining theology offers an important starting place for writing theology.

TAKE A MOMENT TO REFLECT

1. What is your definition of theology? How does this definition impact the way you write theology?

---

9. Merton, *The Sign of Jonas*, 178.

St. Augustine Tangles with Helen's Word

Writers have been complaining that other writers are producing bad prose for centuries. Saint Augustine and Helen Sword both have voiced some major complaints about nonfiction prose. People don't like to read poorly written materials. It is painful. Augustine, who lived in the fourth century, was a gifted theologian and preacher who became a bishop in North Africa. Helen Sword is an associate professor at the University of Auckland, New Zealand, and argues for stylish academic writing. On the surface, these two don't seem to have much in common. But despite the centuries that separate them, they both make many of the same arguments on the need for good writing.

Saint Augustine, in his fourth book within *On Christian Teaching* finished in 427 CE, devotes several pages to arguing that theologians need to write well in order to "win over the antagonistic, rouse the apathetic, and make clear to those who are not conversant with the matter under discussion what they should expect."[10] While in *Stylish Academic Writing,* Helen Sword argues that "elegant ideas deserve elegant expression; that intellectual creativity thrives best in an atmosphere of experimentation rather than conformity; and that, even within the constraints of disciplinary norms, most academics enjoy a far wider range of stylistic choices than they realize."[11]

Bad writing is nothing new. People have complained about boring, confusing, tedious, and bewildering prose for centuries, but writers like Augustine and Sword have also been around for centuries, calling writers to do a better job. Augustine spells it out very simply when he writes "surely, then, the art of speaking both eloquently and wisely is a matter of using adequate words, in the restrained style, striking words in the mixed style, and powerful words in the grand style."[12] Sword describes most academic prose as "impersonal, stodgy, jargon-laden, abstract prose that ignores or defies most of the stylistic principles."[13] She notes that good writers "take care to remain intelligible to educated readers both within and beyond their own disciplines, they think hard about *how* and *what* they write, and they resist intellectual conformity. Above all, they never get dressed in the dark."[14]

10. Augustine, *On Christian Teaching,* 103.

11. Sword, *Stylish Academic Writing,* vii.

12. Augustine, *On Christian Teaching,* 144.

13. Sword, *Stylish Academic Writing,* 3.

14. Ibid., viii.

Both Augustine and Sword develop three major objectives for good, nonfiction prose. Augustine writes: "so these three aims, that the audience understand, delight, and obey—must be sought in this style too, where delight is paramount."[15] Sword's three major factors of stylish prose are communication, craft, and creativity. These six factors of good writing, which are very much related, furnish more than enough to start a writing revolution. Understanding, delight, and obedience, along with communication, craft, and creativity empower theology to be the best that it can be.

Augustine's understanding and Sword's communication both deal with the writer's ability to convey ideas through their prose to readers. These are critical factors for writers. Your audience comes first. If people don't understand your ideas and arguments, all is lost. Readers matter! Augustine notes that writers "should not speak in such a way as that they set themselves up as similar authorities, themselves in need of exposition, but should endeavor first and foremost in all their sermons to make themselves understood and to ensure, by means of the greatest possible clarity, that only the very slow fail to understand."[16] For Sword, "communication implies respect for one's audience."[17] Good narrative requires writers to provide clear, concise texts that readers can understand. Know your readers and write for them. Well-written theology shouldn't need an interpreter to tell readers what the author means.

Delight and craft are also related. Not only do readers need to be able to understand what writers mean, they deserve to enjoy what they are reading. Augustine's delight focuses on the reader while Sword's craft focuses on the writer, but both relate to the quality of the prose itself. Sword identifies craft as "respect for language."[18] She explains that "a carefully crafted sentence welcomes its reader like a comfortable rocking chair, bears its readers across chasms like a suspension bridge, and helps its reader navigate tricky terrain like a well-hewn walking stick."[19] Great writers spend the time and effort to produce outstanding sentences that fit together like pieces of a puzzle forming a beautiful picture. Augustine writes that "well written [words] tend not only to be read on first acquaintance, but also to be reread with considerable pleasure by those who are already acquainted

15. Augustine, *On Christian Teaching*, 142.

16. Ibid., 114–15.

17. Sword, *Stylish Academic Writing*, 173.

18. Ibid., 173.

19. Ibid., 48.

with and have not yet lost their memory of them." He continues by writing that "learning has a lot in common with eating: to cater for the dislikes of the majority even the nutrients essential to life must be made appetizing."[20] Similarly, when Sword asked seventy academics how stylish academic writers write, she found they want writers to:

- express complex ideas clearly and precisely;
- produce elegant, carefully crafted sentences;
- convey a sense of energy, intellectual commitment, and even passion;
- engage and hold their reader's attention;
- tell a compelling story;
- avoid jargon,
- provide their readers with aesthetic and intellectual pleasure;
- and write with originality, imagination, and creative flair.[21]

Delight and craft are about giving pleasure to our readers. These concepts demonstrate the need for offering readers a great reading experience that brings them back to reread because they enjoyed the story.

Augustine's final concept for good theology is obedience. Obedience is not a concept that many people seem to like, but it is critical to well-written theology. Augustine's obedience does not mean unquestioning loyalty and blind acceptance; rather, his obedience captures the sense of being trustworthy and believable. Augustine instructs writers to do their homework. Readers need to be able to trust you as a writer. They need to believe that you are not misleading them, tricking them, or giving them bad advice. Readers need to be able to trust that you did your research, that your words can be trusted, and that your ideas are worth listening to. Theologians need to convince their readers to invite obedience.

Sword's concept of creativity is similar to Augustine's obedience. She uses this concept to mean respect for the "academic endeavor."[22] This doesn't mean writing like everyone else. It doesn't mean producing dry, boring prose that strings together a lot of meaningless words; rather, creativity means having enough passion and commitment to do it right. To do the research, do the grunt work of checking citations, spend hours edit-

---

20. Augustine, *On Christian Teaching*, 117.

21. Sword, *Stylish Academic Writing*, 8.

22. Ibid., 173.

ing and revising to create prose that you are proud to share, that embodies creativity. Sword explains, "some stylish academics . . . communicate such an intense, almost giddy pleasure in and through their writing that only the most curmudgeonly of readers could fail to be carried along with it."[23] If it is worth writing, if it is worth being published, then it is worth the time and effort. Respect for the academic endeavor earns writers the respect of readers. Readers appreciate creative prose. They might not agree with everything you write, but they will acknowledge the scholarship, commitment, and passion that went into it. They will learn that they can trust your work. That they don't need to double check your quotes. That you are not trying to hide your motives and beliefs. That you worked hard to make this a great reading experience for them.

Beautiful, Compelling, and Engaging

Building on the work of Helen Sword and Augustine, I believe that the three most critical elements for well-written theology are that it be engaging, compelling, and beautiful. These three concepts are deeply linked. Well-written theology may be beautiful and still fail to be compelling and engaging, while some of the most engaged theology may be written in ugly prose that readers find baffling and repulsive.

First, I propose the concept of engagement. The argument that theology is idle speculation that achieves nothing but reinforcement of the existing belief patterns of people who only believe what they want to believe has been around for decades. Theology is too often only about abstract ideas. An engaged theology is grounded in the tangible.[24] Theologians can write about all of the classical theological categories, such as pneumatology, soteriology, and eschatology, without floating off into the stratosphere. Engagement ties the theology narrative to the world through examples and stories, keeping its feet on the ground. Without engagement, theological categories are nothing but half-dead, zombiefied concepts buried beneath a stone that will never be rolled away. But together they are the living, breathing Reign of God. They are faith in action. They are the blocks of theology, a theology that builds bridges between the world of ideas and the world of human experience. Karl Barth, a great twentieth-century Swiss theologian, recalled the advice he gave a young theologian during an interview with *Time*

23. Ibid., 163.
24. Wilobee, *The Write Stuff*, 89.

magazine: "take your Bible and take your newspaper, and read both. But interpret newspapers from your Bible."[25] This statement reminds theologians that they live in this world. Theology is not just about the sweet by-and-by, but takes place in the world and must respond to the world's realities. Our theology must care about the events taking place in our hometowns and on the other side of the globe. Using engaged theological approaches creates sticky knowledge that keeps stories and lessons in the minds and hearts of generations to come. After all, what is a parable without an ear to hear it?

Compelling, my second concept, means grabbing and holding our readers' attention. This concept again deals with readers' experience of the text. Compelling narratives drive their readers to do something: keep reading and hopefully be inspired to re-read the text. They build arguments that appeal to the head, the heart, and the soul. The Rev. Charles Adams offered a powerful example of compelling theological prose at the funeral of Rosa Parks. The prayer not only celebrated the life and work of the Mother of the Civil Rights Movement, but also compels readers to listen again and to act. Adams utilizes a variety of writing techniques to compel his readers: storytelling, concrete details, apaphora, homoioteleution, and personification, just to name a few. These techniques generate a powerful listening experience for his audience. To get the full effect, listen to this prayer on YouTube.

He prays, "Lord God, our dwelling place and all generations, we praise you for the victory of Christ that is made manifest to all in the quiet defiance of Rosa Parks. In her smiling life we see your gracious face; we feel your amazing love. In her humble name we hear the echoing vibrations of your excellent name and nature, as her name represents the powers of the weak, your name communicates the humanity and the humility of the ultimate power."[26] Note the concrete details, strong action verbs, and powerful sounds and cadence of the prose.

He continues with compelling storytelling full of conflict and tension as he recounts her experience. He prays,

> We praise you because she found a seat to sit on and she stayed in that seat and with your word and your living Christ she moved the entire universe closer to justice, love, and peace. We praise you today because you gave her all she needed just to keep her seat. You made her keep her seat on row 11 behind 10 rows reserved for whites. She sat on the aisle seat, next to her sat a man nearest

25. "Barth in Retirement," 60.

26. Adams, "Prayer at the Funeral of Rosa Parks." C-SPAN video.

the window on the right hand side of the bus facing forward. Next to her there were two black men sitting in their seats. But oh God it was you, nobody but you that the black men got up and moved when told to do so, a black woman got up and moved, but Rosa Parks kept her seat. . . . She sat down; she sat down, so that we might sit in higher seats. And because she sat down where she sat we are now sitting in the House of Congress, sitting on the Supreme Court, sitting as presidents and CEO's of global corporations, heads of Ivy-league schools, pastors of mega churches, Secretary of States, sitting at the table where cosmic decisions are made. . . . Custom said get up, society said get up, history said get up, the law said get up, Uncle Tom politics said get up, the bus driver growled get up, the police men and the sheriff said get up, but she sat down because you gave her the power to defy an unjust law . . . she took away all of the strength of Jim Crow. Jim Crow had to cough up blood acerbity had to move out of the way.

His language is concrete and filled with real life examples, images, and prophetic messages that make those who listen fellow pilgrims on the quest to carry on this divine work. Compelling theology hooks a reader and doesn't let go. Even when the readers have put down the book, compelling theology keeps them thinking about its ideas and implications.

My third precept, beauty, refers to the prose itself. For me, this beauty links to Augustine's concept of delight and Sword's concept of craft. Beauty happens when writers take the time to carefully craft their prose to make it a great reading experience for their readers. Beauty goes beyond simple respect for language to an understanding of language as an art. Beautiful theology calls its readers to sit in wonder as they draw nearer to God and other humans through words. Readers will return again and again to beautiful theology, finding layers of meaning, new insights, and enjoyment every time they reread it. To write beautiful theology, writers must work sentence by sentence, sometimes word by word, writing and rewriting to allow their readers to marvel at the complexity and simplicity of the story. A good narrative is simple to understand, but complexity blooms in each reader's interpretation. Beautiful theology may be poetic or precise, but it must be powerful.

Theologians Stephen Pattison and James Woodward write what I consider a beautiful theological sentence: "flowers are transitory, but this contributes to their value rather than negating it!"[27] What an amazing

---

27. Pattison and Woodward, "A Vision of Pastoral Theology," 43.

sentence. This sentence forces the reader to stop and reflect. Its meaning is very simple. Flowers are only around for a short time. They bloom and die, but this makes them more valuable, not less. The complexity of the idea, coupled with the compound structure of the sentence, which starts with a simple statement followed by a twist that combines strong verb choice and good diction, results in a powerful, beautiful reading experience.

TAKE A MOMENT TO REFLECT

1. What three adjectives would you select to describe your theological writing?
2. What three adjectives do you want readers to give when talking about your writing?

I hope you feel compelled to keep reading past this first chapter. In the next two chapters we unpack the concept of engagement and invite you to consider the implications of this concept in writing theology. Revolutions can be fun! Let's shake things up.

An Epistle to Undergraduate Students Starting
on Their Journey

Dear Brothers and Sisters,

Welcome! You are coming to theology at a very exciting time. I was an English education major as an undergraduate, which is when I fell in love with great prose. But though I wasn't a theology major, I want to encourage you as you embark on your journey into the undergraduate study of theology.

Before you begin to break the rules, I encourage you to learn them first. Master the English sentence. Study writing: creative writing, business writing, non-fiction, composition, poetry. Study all forms and techniques of writing. Listen and ask. Get feedback and re-write. Avoid anyone who wants you to write as they write.

Ask your professors what kind of writing they want. If they are open to experimenting, try new styles and voices. For those professors who only want to read the standard academic paper, master the style and give them what they want. In the end, this helps you too. Learning to write within a set of rules forces you to examine each and every element of your writing. It helps you become precise, and forces you to consider your intended reader. There will be many writing projects that require you to make a particular reader or editor happy before it is ready to be published.

My second piece of advice is to read. Read economics, read biology, read old novels, read postmodern thrillers, read poetry, read the Bible. Always keep a book with you, whether print or digital. I feel what novelist Stephen King argues is very true: "the more you read, the less apt you are to make a fool of yourself with your pen or word processor."[1] Read not only for content; read for writing style. Read Scripture as a spiritual exercise and

1. King, *On Writing*, 150.

an academic study. Learn how to read research. Read tradition. Talk about what you are reading; share your ideas and bring your sources into conversation with each other. Understand that each and every class you take (not just your theological classes) offers you opportunities to grow as a reader and theologian. If you don't have enough time to read, you'll never be able to write engaged, compelling, and beautiful theology. Make the time.

Next, go out and *do* theology. Theologian Laurie Green explains that "time was when students would go to college or university to 'read' theology rather than 'do' theology."[2] We all need to *do* theology and not just in the classroom, but in the parish, in the wider culture—from farm fields to corporate offices. Theology is a contact sport. It requires you to be out in the world not locked up in a room with only your books for company. But didn't I just tell you to make time to read? There is a skill in finding balance. Theologian C. S. Song explains that "God is not a concept; God is story. God is not idea; God is presence. God is not hypothesis; God is experience. . . . What is the best way to gain access to this God? Surely not by means of concepts, ideas, hypotheses, or principles, but by means of the life we live, the experiences we go through, in a word, by means of the stories we weave, the stories we tell and share."[3] Go out there! Do theology and add experience to what you read. Sit down and share your insights with the people around you. Gain insights. But remember this sharing doesn't need to be a debate. We have enough religious fights and competition. Share and be open to listen. Listening doesn't mean agreeing. Start with reading and listening.

As you are doing theology, write, write, and write. Writing will empower you to pay attention and think about what happens around you. Keep journals, write poetry, respond to what you read and capture your thoughts and impressions. The more you write the better your writing will become. Unpack your mind on the page or the screen. Connect the dots between your faith and the rest of the world. Write essays to build bridges between the sacred and the secular and from the secular to the sacred. Learn how to write with sources. And learn to give your sources credit for their hard work. Remember the commandment: do not steal and learn to cite. Master the concept that research is not simply rewriting other people's ideas. Even in your personal journal make citations to help you remember that source. You will feel terrible years later, when you reread your journal,

2. Green, *Let's Do Theology*, 4.

3. Song, *In the Beginning were Stories*, 7.

rediscover a great quote, but then don't know where to find it again for your bibliography. Leave yourself a trail. Research requires you to craft something new based on or inspired by other writers' concepts. Writing with research is like building with blocks—you have the pieces; it's your job to make something of them.

Begin to improve your writing with small projects. Write an essay with a small word limit, or in a form of poetry that forces you to count syllables. Use fixed structures or rhythm. Each of these short projects will force you to craft your writing word by word. When we work word by word, we learn more about our writing than we can from composing a whole book. Once you master small projects, remember that big projects are just a series of small, interrelated projects. A big project is just putting the small pieces together. Often, when we begin a big project, we fall into mediocre writing habits. Mediocre writing might be faster and easier, but it is never better. Do your best to write engaged, compelling, and beautiful theology. You can do this! In regards to theology, remember that doubt is not only normal, it is healthy. Faith without doubt is zombie faith. Each of our lived experiences of faith comes with baggage, but we need to learn how to carry that baggage. Dealing with our baggage empowers us to deal with other people's baggage when we encounter it. Also, remember that theology is important. As theologians Breenan Hill, Paul Knitter, and William Madges remind us, "theology is neither thoughtless chatter nor a monologue."[4] Theology exists as an ongoing conversation that will never come to a definitive end, at least in this existence. It is a conversation from the point of views of faith, and it is vital for the church and the world. Write engaged, compelling, and beautiful theology.

Finally, *keep your feet on the ground.*

---

4. Hill et al., *Faith, Religion, & Theology,* 286–87.

two

Engaged Theology: Yourself

Welcome to the pilgrimage into engaged theology. In the last chapter, I argue effective theology should be engaging, compelling, and beautiful. Theology does not need to be abstract, dull, boring, tedious, dense, inconsequential, trivial, remote, immaterial, or unimportant. Reading theology should not require a PhD. Writing engaged theology just requires planning before you sit down to write a single word. An engaged theology keeps its feet on the ground and in the here and now. This chapter explores the foundation for an engaging theology. Imagine this chapter as a (pre) pre-writing exercise, what you need to do before you start writing.

When you plan a trip, you need to get ready. You don't just jump in a car and show up at the airport without a ticket or destination. Trips require planning. So does writing. To write engaged theology, you need to prepare yourself: spiritually, emotionally, intellectually, and physically. We'll start this prep work with ourselves as theologians and work our way to our sources. To write engaged theology, theologians need a grounded sense of *themselves* and of *the sources for their content*. This chapter explores theological authorship as a (pre) pre-writing requirement. The next chapter addresses the sources for an engaged theology.

Theology has an image problem. When theologians write theology that fails to capture who they are, they contribute to this problem. Theology that comes across in a disconnected and abstract fashion, that only takes place in the realm of ideas and concepts, and that fails to connect theological discourse to the world, its peoples, and its problems, becomes reduced to idle chatter. Writing an engaging theology that has its feet on the ground addresses this problem. Prolific author and farmer Wendell Berry argues that "we are still exactly as dependent on the earth as the earthworms."[1] As theological writers, we depend on life, heaven, earth, and everything in between. We are as dependent as earthworms in our search for meaning and expression. Life provides examples, illustrations, and sources. Keeping your feet on the ground encourages you to allow everyday life to resonate through your theology because everyday life is theological. Life is theology in motion. Life isn't just an illustration for our theology; it is theology.

But we all need to learn how to crawl before we tunnel into writing engaged theology. We have to learn about ourselves. We need to own our reality and identity.

Owning It: You Are a Theologian

You are a theologian. Get over it. Stop stressing about it. Quit hiding it. All Christians are theologians.[2] Expressing engaging theology can be accomplished in many ways, but before you write one word of theology, you must understand yourself as a theologian. There are different types of theologians, and theologians assume many different roles. The theologians who reflect upon themselves as theologians, upon their metaphoric understanding, upon the type of theology they want to write, and upon their role as theologians is miles ahead of someone who gushes out a hundred pages of random, shallow ideas without self-reflection or engagement.

Knowing what type of theology you are writing is very important. Theology takes many forms. Just add the word theology to any of the following: historical, systematic, contextual, process, feminist, womanist, Black, liturgical, Hispanic, Latino/a, LGBT, mystical, comparative, practical, pastoral, liberation, spiritual, biblical, natural, dogmatic, relational (the love-child of process and feminist theologies), and on and on. Each type comes with certain expectations and methodological approaches that you need to map out for yourself as a theological author. This doesn't mean that you are going to follow all of these rules, but it does require you to understand them. If you are going to defy the rules, you should have a rationale and a plan. Never allow yourself to be pigeon-holed as a writer of theology, or as theologian Thomas Merton recommends to poets, "let us remain outside 'their' categories."[3] Theologians must challenge and break down barriers

1. Berry, *The Long-Legged House*, 77.
2. Stone and Duke, *How to Think Theologically*, 1.
3. Merton, *Echoing Silence*, 201.

between categories to write engaged theology. Don't just be content as a specialist who only knows everything about one small sub-subject; rather, mix and blend, empower creativity and outside-of-the-box visions across many subjects. Theology needs visionary words that seek inspiration for insights from the most unlikely sources and in the strangest places. You will not find these unlikely sources and strange places just reading and writing within one small subcategory. Don't just say "my area is theology of work; Civil Rights is outside my scope." Or "I am an ecclesiologist; I don't deal with food! Go talk to the sacramental theologians." Break out of your box!

This implies that, as Thomas Merton writes, "instead of multiplying a Babel of esoteric and technical tongues which isolate men [or women] in their specialties,"[4] theologians build bridges that bring people together by relying on accessible and concrete language. Engaged theological writing, like the poet Merton describes, refuses academic classification. Don't accept someone else's classification of you. Don't allow yourself to become trapped behind a mask that someone placed upon you, alienating you from yourself and your readers. Merton explains that "alienation begins when culture divides me against myself, puts a mask on me, gives me a role I may or may not want to play. Alienation is complete when I become completely identified with my mask, totally satisfied with my role, and convince myself that any other identity or role is inconceivable."[5] You are the theologian and you must be honest to God and yourself. Writing theology is a vocation, not a money-making venture. Theologian, understand yourself. Dig deep and don't stop, even if it hurts. Never write theology for your own gratification or to satisfy ambitions. Write theology to help you understand your faith better and to empower others to understand and express their own faith.

The Many Faces of Theology

There are many roles that theologians assume, including poet, prophet, preacher, storyteller, teacher, translator, "professional" resource, and friend-of-the-soul. Each of these roles is critical for healthy theology, and each theologian should discern what type of role they take on with each writing project. Engaged theology needs each of these roles.

The poet takes theological language and cuts, shapes, distills it. A gifted theological poet can send shockwaves across a reader's mind. The

4. Ibid, 64.

5. Ibid., 71–72.

poet catches a theological insight and distills it again and again until it reaches the highest possible proof the reader can consume. With a few choice words, the poet captures an ocean of insight. Poetic words cut like a knife. Good poetry throws all the rules out the window, shocking, stunning, and pulling the reader from the heights of heaven to the depths of the Mariana Trench under the Pacific Ocean with a single verse. Theological poets compose liturgy, lyrics, and prayers. They take dull theological prose and transform the experience of reading it. They create phrases and images that penetrate into readers' minds and souls. They capture us and make us recall their images long after we forget everything else.

Australian theologian Terry Veling writes, "the poetic word breaks open, energizes, and restores."[6] He explains that "poetry alters our relation to language. In poetry, the uncanny—the strange, the hidden, the unsayable—bring us up short such as we 'undergo an experience of language.'"[7] The theological poet engages language to rip apart and build up. Engaging, compelling, beautiful theological poetry moves the soul to action. Theology needs its poets.

Another role for the theological writer is that of prophet. Prophets have had a larger than life role since biblical times. They speak to power. Prophets don't tell the future; they read the signs of the times and tell people what is really going on in the world. Prophets recognize what is and speak out for what ought to be. Prophets are those few individuals who "dedicate themselves in a special way to living out the full consequences and implications of what they believe."[8] A prophet cries out to heaven for justice, and they live justice. They see ten times as much reality as the rest of us, and they work to open our eyes to this reality. Divine inspiration drives a prophet to speak out. Prophets come from all walks of life and backgrounds; they employ all forms of expression, from righteous anger to jokes that cut deep; and they speak to whoever will listen and those who refuse to listen. The prophet speaks against complacency on behalf of God. They live as social critics who cry out for justice against evil that harms God's creations and will not be silenced by criticism, being fired from a job, or being locked behind the bars of a jail cell. A good prophetic voice makes even "good" Christians feel uncomfortable. Prophets often offend; they do

---

6. Veling, *Practical Theology*, 195.

7. Ibid., 198.

8. Merton, *Echoing Silence*, 74.

what it takes. Sometimes, we need a Chicken Little to tell us that the sky is falling. Theology needs its prophets.

The preacher seems a fairly common theological role, but the church has never had enough "good" preachers. The theological expression of a preacher makes the message palatable, readable, understandable, and sweeter. The preacher's words are generally not as raw or harsh as the prophet's, or as distilled as the poet's, but they are no less powerful; they simply demonstrate a different kind of power. Preachers have pulpits, and they proclaim the good news and share stories that uplift, while shedding light on problems of the church and the world. They foster understanding—the "aha" moment. Preachers produce sermons weekly. After you add special services like Christmas Eve and Holy Thursday, the average preacher writes a book a year. Take this over a career, and a preacher writes the equivalent of around thirty to forty books. Preachers are theology's most prolific authors. The theological preacher is never just an office. He or she must always be in community with other people on this journey called life, willing to share the message even if it does not need words. Theology needs its preachers.

The next theological role never seems to get the credit it deserves. Theological storytellers build stories: novels, short stories, parables, nonfiction, and sermon illustrations. Theologian Daniel Taylor writes that "stories engage us from the tops of our heads to the bottom of our feet and all points in between. Stories transcend our categories. They reject any too-neat division of human beings into intellect, emotion, body, and soul. Stories seize us in our entirety, making equal and integrated appeal to all that we are. Stories make us think, make us feel and imagine, enlarge or diminish our souls, and play a tune on our bodies."[9] Great theological storytellers weave images that show rather than tell. They invite readers to enter a work through their imagination rather than their intellect. Readers always seem to remember the stories, just ask any preacher. Anytime a theological storyteller feels that they are not getting the credit they deserve, they should reflect on the master storyteller: Jesus. The parables of Jesus are all stories—creative, multi-dimensional stories. Stories seem to be Jesus' favorite medium for theology, or at least Jesus' stories are what people remembered enough to record and put into the Gospels. Almost everyone loves a good story. I said *almost* all because as a writer you will never please everyone. Don't try. Theology needs its storytellers.

9. Taylor, *Creating a Spiritual Legacy*, 14.

The roles of a theological teacher and theological translator are critical. Teachers are incredibly patient writers who will explain a concept a dozen different ways because they know that readers learn slowly. A teacher unpacks the concepts with care and patience. Teachers encourage the reader to engage and explore. They don't mind answering stupid questions: over and over, again and again. They don't care if they already explained the concept. Teachers want their readers to learn no matter how hard it makes their writing process. Theology needs its teachers.

The theological translator is a gifted scholar who has the talent of taking insider speech and translating it into everyday lingo. According to Augustine, good writing not only delights, it also teaches, but modern readers also find Augustine very hard to read and understand. Great theological translators can take the most dense, academic jargon and present their readers with clear, concise text. Meaning often emerges from individual words. Translators rescue ideas from the complexity and context of their writers, bringing them to readers in language those readers can understand.

A translator also crafts words to fit the meaning that was left behind by the flow of time. As Edith Bajema explains, "in 1934, the fat *Webster's Dictionary* contained about 450,000 words. By 1978, lexicographers guessed that perhaps 150,000 of the original 450,000 words were still in use. Meanwhile, particularly in the 1960s, more than 200,000 new words invaded the language."[10] Changes in language make older texts hard to understand for today's readers. A translator keeps the language and meaning of a classic accessible to modern audiences. The translator also crosses boundaries and barriers to find gems in other languages, religious traditions, or ages of the faith. Theology needs its translators.

The concept of a theologian as a "professional" resource grows out of the conviction that all Christians are theologians. I place the word "professional" in quotations because I feel that it has been historically misused in theology. For most of Christian history, theological writing was restricted to educated and ordained male elites. Women were mostly excluded from both of these until quite recently.[11] I feel that anyone who has demonstrated their mastery of theology, whether through classroom or lived learning, is a professional theologian. Mastery does not mean that someone hangs up a sign as a guru. British economist Lynda Gratton explains that mastery

10. Bajema, "The Use of Language in Worship," 796.
11. Holmes, "Introduction: Mending a Broken Lineage," 3.

normally requires at least 10,000 hours of practice time.[12] In other words, mastery requires the dedication of a full-time job, forty hours a week, for around five years.

"Professional" resource theologians empower others to articulate and explore their own theological expressions. They act as a hybrid, a human-book, representing years of struggle and learning culled from tradition, Scripture, and research in order to listen, ask non-leading questions, and sometimes even record the group's theology. The resource theologian brings theologies to light. When people want information, the "professional" theologian does the grunt work of research and brings it back to the group, which then shapes and uses it to inform theological expression. "Professional" resource theologians have the gift of empowering others to successfully express their theological gifts.

But this doesn't mean that the "professional" resource theologian reshapes local theology into their own image. Allowing a theologian to dominate the development of a local theology only forces a new hegemony onto already oppressed communities.[13] Hegemony means domination or manipulation by a powerful outside group to control. The "professional" theologian serves as a resource who gently weaves local theological expressions with Scripture, tradition, experience, and research. And then brings the theological text back to the local community to ask them if they got it right. The "professional" resource theologian always needs the affirmation of the community theologians whose ideas were used to affirm this content authentically represents them. Theology needs its "professional" resource theologians.

The final role that I want to explore in this section is the friend-of-the-soul. A friend-of-the-soul lives as a writer of theology who pilgrimages with their readers. They inspire, comfort, and bring hope. They remind us that we are not alone on this journey of faith. This role invites readers to join the author, whether sitting quietly among the pine trees or on a quest of self-discovery. I believe that Anne Lamott captures this role when she writes,

> writing and reading decrease our sense of isolation. They deepen and widen and expand our sense of life: they feed the soul. When writers make us shake our heads with the exactness of their prose and their truths, and even make us laugh about ourselves or life,

12. Gratton, *The Shift*, 63.
13. Schreiter, *Constructing Local Theologies*, 18.

our buoyancy is restored. We are given a shot at dancing with, or at least clapping along with, the absurdity of life, instead of being squashed by it over and over again. It's like singing on a boat during a terrible storm at sea. You can't stop the raging storm, but singing can change the hearts and spirits of the people who are together on that ship.[14]

Friends-of-the-soul are fellow pilgrims, writing and inviting readers to join them on an exploration or to simply be. They are not guides, spiritual masters, or gurus, but companions that remind readers that we aren't alone. Theology needs its friends-of-the-soul.

These are not the only roles theologians assume when they write. There are many other roles, such as evangelist, musician, pastor, artist, social critic, chaplain, and sage. The key for you, the theological writer, is in reflecting on the role that you are engaging when working on a particular piece of writing. Don't isolate these roles from each other—mix, blend, create hybrids from them. Become a poet/friend-of-the-soul, a preacher/teacher, or an unemployed but brilliant prophet/translator. Or assume a mantle that I haven't considered or dreamed of in these passages. Know yourself, theologian. Engage your role. Empower yourself to plan your pilgrimage of writing engaged theology by engaging yourself.

TAKE A MOMENT TO REFLECT

1. Are any of these roles attractive to you? Which ones? Why?
2. Is there one of these roles that you could never imagine yourself being? Why?

Don't Pretend to be Neutral

Engaged theology needs theologians to engage. Some theologians seem to believe that we can be bystanders, detached observers, innocent and without responsibility, but this is not true. Theologian Martyn Percy recounts a parable in his book: "the artist swims in the sea, but the critic stands on the shore."[15] Theologians must swim in the sea of faith to articulate theology.

14. Lamott, *Bird by Bird*, 237.
15. Percy, *Engaging with Contemporary Culture*, 7.

They cannot stand on the shore and offer insight. You cannot offer insight if you do not understand what is happening, and you cannot understand what is happening unless you experience it. Theologians must enter the waters of life. They cannot be isolated, they cannot be watchers, and they cannot be critics on the shore.

Once you enter the waters of life you are not a bystander, not a detached observer, not without responsibility. Theologians must live life, and life is messy. It is complicated. It is emotional. It is illogical. You must experience faith to write about faith; faith with all of its crises, valleys, dead-ends, and one-way streets. You must experience both mountain-top and valley faith. This is not a neutral theology. If you are living life, you are going to have feelings and convictions about what is happening. When we swim in the sea of faith, we open ourselves, both as theologians and writers, to the possibility of change. We will not emerge the same as when we entered. We are changed by our experiences. Theologian C. S. Song argues that "a neutral theology is a homeless theology" that doesn't belong anywhere.[16] Theologians take a stand; they acknowledge their biases and write from their own experiences, Scriptures, and religious traditions. In other words, they must build a home for themselves. They must write their own contexts. Context is very important for writers of theology. Our context is where we are. Theologians must be part of the context that they are attempting to write about. They must be invested in what is happening around them. Engaged theology not only begins in its own context, it keeps its feet firmly planted on the ground of its context. Theologian William Willimon explains that "most good writers cling closely to the solid stuff of earth."[17] Good writers cling to the concrete instead of floating off into the abstract. Understanding that you aren't writing neutral theology impacts both your writing style and your content.

This knowledge forces theologians to write in their own theological voice and style. We don't all speak alike; therefore, we should not all write alike. We must be ourselves when we write theology. Our theological writing styles should be as individualistic as our own experiences. As Judson Edwards explains, "no one can bleed your blood onto the page. Your subject matter may not be unique, but your perspective and writing style will be."[18] When you write theology in your own style, you build trust with

16. Song, *Tell Us Our Names*, 11.
17. Willimon, *Reading with Deeper Eyes*, 12.
18. Edwards, *Blissful Affliction*, 93.

your readers. You demonstrate your honesty. Helen Sword encourages her readers "to adopt whatever stylistic strategies best suit their own skin. Stylish academic writing can be serious, entertaining, straightforward, poetic, unpretentious, ornate, intimate, impersonal, and much in between."[19] You must write from your own skin. You must learn to be comfortable in your own skin, in your own style, in your own calling.

Secondly, this impacts your theological content. There is no need to pretend you are something else. We shouldn't write about concepts that we've never experienced. You should not write about the dark night of the soul if you have not endured a dark night of the soul. Your content must reflect who and what you are. You engage examples from your own life, not from the other side the world. Why write about something from outside your context? It only leaves you open to misinterpretation. When you see or hear something from outside your culture and then write about it, you risk missing a key aspect, of misunderstanding, or not having the perspective to provide effective theological engagement.

Theologians are not heroes of the faith, and we are not spiritual masters with all the answers. But theologians do offer their readers content that is not neutral. Theologians ask questions. We come with biases, embedded theologies, and preconceived positions. As theologians Howard Stone and James Duke note, "our embedded theology may seem so natural and feel so comfortable that we carry it within us for years, unquestioned and perhaps even unspoken except when we join in the words of others at worship."[20] Our embedded theology is like a pair of glasses. The lens shapes what we see and how we interpret what we see. Our embedded theology grows out of lived experiences that start from infancy. It is formed by the songs our parents and grandparents sing to us, shaped by the stories told by those people we admire, and controlled by our experience of growing up in a particular time and place.

Writing a non-neutral theology requires putting it all on the table: our presuppositions, our biases, and our embedded theology, and labeling it for what it is. This means that in our theological style and content we are not only true to ourselves as authors, we are honest with our readers. We proclaim that ours is not a neutral theology. This requires theologians to make their part in the stories apparent. Don't hide from your readers or

19. Sword, *Stylish Academic Writing*, viii.
20. Stone and Duke, *How to Think Theologically*, 16.

pretend there are no elephants in the room. The biggest elephant in the room is power, and it's your job to make it known.

You Have Power: Own It

Understanding yourself as a theologian requires reflecting on power. Theologian Laurie Green, a bishop in the Church of England, writes "in the actual *doing* of theology we must be alert to the questions of power—it must be a shared community affair, open to all and not in the hands of any elite group."[21] A major element in self-awareness is power. Engaged theology requires that theologians not only see and acknowledge the elephant in the room, but also engage the elephant and others in dialogue about power. Being a published theologian places you and me in a position of power. There exist many types of power at play in theology: male and female; lay and ordained; race; nationality; religious tradition; socio-economic class; sexual orientation; educational level; age; immigration status; employment status; and on and on. You must address your power in the theology you write.

In 1993, author Sherman Alexie published a collection of short stories, *The Lone Ranger and Tonto Fistfight in Heaven,* chronicling the daily experiences on the Spokane Indian Reservation where he grew up. The title of this work always intrigued me. I struggle with the question of the relationship between the stereotypical, white hero riding into town to save the day with *his* minority side-kick to that of the white, male theologian telling a diverse audience of Christian communities how their faith should seek understanding. I have also struggled with the authority and responsibility of my own theological voice as a heterosexual white male in the United States. I have to ask the question of how and even if I can dialogue and produce theology in a room filled with the invisible elephants of power and privilege that exist within a community of brothers and sisters who see and feel the weight of these elephants.

Theologian James Cone reminds the white Christian community that the problem of reconciliation is the oppressor's problem.[22] It is the issue of the white church to find theological solutions around the practices of faith in light of race relations and, most of all, this makes it my issue as a Midwestern, North American, white, heterosexual, upper-middle class,

---

21. Green, *Let's Do Theology*, 12.
22. Cone, *A Black Theology of Liberation*.

economically stable male. I need to figure out how to speak with an authentic theological voice that has value for other men and women from an array of theological, racial, socio-economic, gender, and ethnic contexts, and also be able to discern when my responsibility is to listen and not to speak in silent solidarity. I take this job very seriously. If I want to speak a theology that is valid and usable for a wider Christian community, then I must articulate, come to an understanding with, and engage my power. And you as a writer of theology must do the same.

Language is a very important aspect in the formation of power, especially given the history of whiteness as the norm of experience and truth. Theologian Sheryl Kujawa-Holbrook argues that European American students must use "I" statements in their theology. She writes, "in all cases, teachers and students alike should be encouraged to speak only from the perspective of their own experience using 'I' statements."[23] This usage of the "I" pronoun requires the writer to take a sense of ownership and responsibility for their statements.

But the "I" also has dangers as theologian Miguel De La Torre points out when he writes that "by projecting the 'I' upon the marginalized, those who are of the dominant culture are able to define themselves as worthier of the benefits society has to offer, either because they are more industrious (the Protestant work ethic) or are 'simply wiser.'"[24] This means the use of "I," especially for European/European-American males, must be as a humble pilgrim and not a know-it-all ass. It must be a way for individuals from a dominant culture to define themselves and honor the value of other "I" from other cultures who can teach other ways of knowing and expressing. "I's" are very important, especially when theologians remember to make it the individual "I," not an "I" speaking for the community "we."

This pronoun "I" helps me to articulate ownership and responsibility for my theology. It also encourages my theology to become more than just a history of ideas by embedding personal narrative into a living faith that still seeks an understanding of itself, the world where humanity resides, and the God who created us. I find it sad that many theologians hide their best and most original ideas in footnotes where so many of their audiences never read them. The use of the personal "I" allows me as a theologian to see myself in my theology, and forces me to acknowledge the subjectivity and objectivity that exist within my use of language.

23. Kujawa-Holbrook, "Beyond Diversity," 147.
24. De La Torre, *Doing Christian Ethics from the Margins*, 17.

The use of "I" also aids theologians not only with their side of the conversation, but by reminding theologians who their audience is and should be. Methodist theologian Emmanuel Lartey, who is originally from Ghana, explains that one of his dialogue partners argues that theologians cannot be "all things to all people," and that the solution is to "only speak to one's own reality to a specific, clearly defined audience, preferably of one's own people."[25] But Lartey believes that theologians can address people across barriers of power without re-colonization by the West. He lays out three principles: "contextuality, multiple perspectives, and authentic participation."[26] I agree that a theologian cannot be all things to all people. But when theologians engage other people, ways of knowing, and beliefs with dignity and respect, they can offer theological expression that is useful and meaningful to a wider community.

All of these conversations about power, race, gender, and nationality begin conversations that any theologian must reflect on for themselves. Very often, aspects of power are invisible to those who hold it. When we normalize our experiences, we fail to see our own blind spots and embedded theology. You must ask your own questions and discern your own answers.

I hope that everyone who reads this book is not a white male Protestant. I hope that my choices and work influence a wider audience. By outing myself as a theologian and acknowledging my limitations, I invite my readers to discern what is valuable and useful to them. My reflection on my power helps me respect my audience. Poet John Leax recounts, "when I was a teenager, one of my mother's favorite phrases was, 'it's not what you say, but it's how you say it.' I hated those words, but I understand now, in reminding me to respect my audience, she was teaching me a lesson vital to writing to and for a place, a community. One cannot long disrespect one's neighbors and continue to live in the neighborhood."[27] Or as Max Warren notes that "our first task in approaching another people, another culture, another religion is to take off our shoes, for the place we are approaching is holy."[28] The church doesn't need any more Lone Ranger theologians to ride in to correct and solve everyone's problems. Theologians need to respect other cultures, experiences, and ways of knowing. Theology does not need

25. Lartey, *Pastoral Theology*, 10.
26. Ibid., 11.
27. Leax, "Within Infinite Purposes," 18.
28. Warren, "Introduction," 10.

any more moralizing, scolding, or talking down to other believers. We can share our own version of orthodoxy without beating people up or shaming them. There exists power in the words of written theology, and these words can do great good or great harm. Power comes with responsibility.

Tom Christenson's five temptations of theological discourse provide important insights for theological authors. He warns that people engaged in theological discourse must watch out for the temptation of power:

- that one is saying the last (or the first) word,

- the temptation of power that comes with a higher authority,

- the temptation to not notice how much of our knowledge consists in naming our ignorance,

- the temptation of mistaking linguistic facility for understanding, and

- the temptation to infer ontology from grammar.[29]

This does not require individuals who bring unintended supremacy to the dialogue through their social, cultural, gender, and/or educational status to be silent, but it does require these individuals act out of special awareness that may encourage them to be silent more than they normally do and then to speak mindfully without having the first or the last word.[30] If your theology promotes racism, sexism, elitism, nationalism, or any form of hatred or discrimination, you can call it theology but don't call it Christian.

As writers of theology you have to learn to write "disciplined prose" not "knee-jerk responses."[31] Theologians are not called to manipulate, dominate, or control people. You can disagree with respect. You can teach without re-making people in your own image. And you can still learn important lessons from the most unlikely people in the most unlikely places. The theologian who understands power accepts that with power comes responsibility.

You can address your responsibility in dozens of little ways that add up to making a difference. Many style manuals encourage writers to only label other authors by their family names, but this hides authors' gender. I try to always introduce authors by their full names and to always use their full names in bibliographic entries of their work. Also, I make a conscious effort to make sure my theology engages people of different genders, sexual

29. Christenson, "The Oddest Word," 165–72.

30. Ibid., 182.

31. Merton, *Echoing Silence*, 74.

orientations, races, ethnic groups, and faith traditions. I once read a 485-page book of theology written by a prominent male theologian written in 1991. As I finished, I had a feeling that made me check each and every one of his footnotes. In the over one hundred sources this theologian used for his theology he never engaged one resource by a female theologian or scholar. This made me question his use of power in writing a theology that ignores so many great insights.

TAKE A MOMENT TO REFLECT

1. What elephants are in the room with you as you write theology?
2. What responsibilities come with your power to write theology?

Revel in the Spirit

After you unpack your use of power, you need to consider your spirituality. Writing engaged theology must be a spiritual practice. Writing is a ministry. Theologian Gustavo Gutiérrez writes that "any reflection that does not help in living according to the Spirit is not a Christian theology."[32] Writing engaged theology must be done in a spirit of prayer. It must be formed in the spirit of God in the service of the community. But theologians cannot keep pouring their spiritual lifeblood out onto the page without running dry. Theologians must keep replenishing reserves. An oil lamp cannot burn forever without running dry.

Anglican theologian Laurie Green notes that "the best theology is not so much talk about God, as attaining the habit of knowing we're always in God's presence. To make ourselves 'present to the presence of God' was the whole concern of theology during the earliest times, for you can read theology without praying, but you cannot be a theologian yourself without the habit of prayer and devotion."[33] You, as a theologian, must budget time for spiritual practices that refresh you. This time is as critical as reading, writing, and reflecting. Without taking care of your own spirituality, your theology will be dead: dead words on a page without hope or vision.

32. Gutiérrez, *We Drink From Our Own Wells*, 37.
33. Green, *Let's Do Theology*, 14.

Jesuit theologian Thomas Green fosters spirituality as a contemplative-in-action. His approach empowers spirituality in theological expression; his illustration of the sea and the person demonstrates this. The person who hears and responds to God's call finds the "sea of God." Green believes that there are two basic models of how people exist in the sea of God: as swimmers or as floaters. Swimmers set their own course and rely primarily on their own skill and muscle to get them to their goal.[34] But the floater, who is not passive at all, must respond to "every movement of the wind and the tide," losing control of their own destination and destiny. Green reminds the floaters that they may be the sacraments to the swimmers around them, "for whom the Lord of love waits so patiently."[35] Green's spirituality requires trust in God, as writers are called upon to stop relying on their strength and power. This is not a passive spirituality of writing that just requires the theologian to be in God; rather, it requires the writer to discern the movement of God and allow their body to respond and do God's work. Writing engaged theology should be a process of floating in God's sea. This floating will foster a constant sense of spiritual discernment throughout the writing process. We cannot write engaged theology relying on our own strength.

Take a Moment to Reflect

1. What spiritual practices refill your tank to continue writing engaged theology?
2. Are you a swimmer or a floater? Why?

Together, Alone

Although discernment begins as a process of self-reflection, discernment needs other people. Engaged theology demands other people. You should never write theology alone. Christianity requires community; and writing theology is a communal act. The theologian should not swim or float alone. Writing theology must bring us, as writers, into communion with one another. When theologians write alone, they risk losing touch with the world. It is easy to become lost in the ideas of theology. Writing with a

34. Green, *Darkness in the Marketplace*, 123.
35. Ibid., 128.

group empowers theologians to keep their feet on the ground; it prevents the theology from shooting off on tangents; it stops them from being blown by the latest fad or trend; and it embodies theology as a process of group discernment.

Writing engaged theology must be a process of group discernment. Theologian David Tracy writes,

> to discern suggests an imagery of tentativeness, groping, risk-bearing alertness, that self-exposure of an authentically spiritual sensitivity to the anxieties and fears, the possibilities of both kairotic moments and demonic threats, the refusal to accept timidity in the risk of uncovering the fundamental religious questions in the situation—questions which the very attempt to formulate, however hesitantly, is always worthwhile.[36]

Theological discernment must empower and strengthen the community for the pilgrimage ahead but, like writing, it is a struggle. Discernment captures the sense of spiritual searching and prayerful questions while embedding this searching within a group reminds us that God speaks through others. Other people aid us. Sometimes we are too stubborn to listen to God, but when enough people share the same insights with us, it fosters "aha" moments for God to break through.

Group discernment also prevents a danger of writing theology alone. Writing theology alone opens the door to an overly individualistic approach that may lead you to distort or misinterpret your sources for doing theology. A group of fellow theologians grounds the writer in the here and now. Theological reflection needs to be carried out as dialogical discernment within the local Christian community in light of Scripture and the wider Christian traditions. The process itself must always be transitioning to stay in step with the times, needs, callings, and contexts of theology. A group can open the writer's eyes to other possibilities and avenues for exploration.

On the flip side, there is also a danger in writing within a group. Often in groups there is at least one strong personality that attempts to dominate the message. Do not allow others to remake your theology into their image. Do not allow them to make your voice, your style, your content sound like their's. Consensus does not mean reducing the message to one person's point-of-view. In a spirit of prayer, you must listen to each group member's insights and decide what to change and what to leave alone. After the theological writing process is done, it is still up to the community to open itself

36. Tracy, *The Analogical Imagination*, 339.

in prayer to the transcending power of God. As British theologians John Swinton and Harriet Mowat note "we don't find truth, truth finds us!"[37] Let it find you.

Take this manuscript. I did not write it alone. I deliberately designed the process to foster participation and input from others. First, Gricel Dominguez read and revised each chapter. Next, I e-mailed each chapter to a group of clergy, university faculty, PhD candidates, and graduate students. This wasn't just a random group of people. The group consisted of men and women, laity and ordained, parish clergy and clergy in other settings, people with various levels of formal education, people from many different denominations, and some with no religious background. They come from all around the world: South America, the Caribbean, Asia, Europe, and North America. Each brought unique perspectives and insights to this project. They pointed out what I had missed, assumed, and not explained. Writing engaged theology as a group process of discernment encourages us to listen to the voice of God through others. It allows the process of writing to be embodied with our spirituality.

I hope this chapter has helped you prepare yourself emotionally, intellectually, and spiritually for this pilgrimage. The next chapter encourages you to continue prepping and planning for your journey to write theology.

Now that you have prepared yourself to write theology, it is time to prepare for your pilgrimage. It is time to plan the trip, get your tickets, develop your itinerary, pack your bags.

TAKE A MOMENT TO REFLECT

1. What processes of discernment do you need in your writing?

2. Have you prepared yourself to write theology? How?

---

37. Swinton and Mowat, *Practical Theology*, 254.

three

Engaged Theology: Your Sources

I have to admit, I put writing this chapter off until the end. Even as I write this chapter, I realize every other chapter has already gone through two or more drafts. Why? Because I'm human, and I don't like to attempt dangerous and arduous tasks. Engaging the sources of theology seems hard. Trying to cover what many authors write whole volumes about feels daunting. These aren't just little books, but large, dense tomes that can serve as a door stop. Theologian John Thiel observes, "the notion that theology has 'sources' is a relatively recent one in the history of theological thinking."[1] But recognizing that theology *does* have sources has been an important step in the development of theological thinking. Engaged theology requires writers to reach out and grapple with Scripture, tradition, experience, and research as sources. This isn't easy, which is why so many theologians focus on one of the four and breeze over the others in passing. Engaged theology depends on the writer engaging all of these sources.

Now that you have prepared yourself to go on a writing pilgrimage into the world of engaged theology by engaging *yourself* as a theologian, you need to plan your trip: how you are going to get there and what are you going to do? You need maps and guides, sources for theological reflection—Scripture, experience, tradition, and research. In the previous chapter, we learned about ourselves and how to prepare for the journey. It is like learning to use your hands, your feet, and your head (all at once) while driving. Now, we need to plan the route we'll take to get to your destination. Are we traveling along expressways or down country roads? What will we do if we reach a dead-end? Or end up in a cow pasture greeted by an angry

1. Thiel, *Imagination & Authority*, 204.

bull? You need to read travel guides and map out the best routes to reach your destination, but you also need to be ready for the unexpected turns and roadblocks you might encounter when the spirit leads you in a different direction. Remember, as Sarah Stockton warns us, "the pilgrim's path cannot be mapped beforehand. It moves toward the sacred with twists and turns unique to you alone."[2] We like to plan, though it often seems that God likes to turn all our careful planning on its head. Be ready for *anything* and plan for *everything*, that's writing.

Sources for Theological Reflection

Sources for theological reflection exist all around us. Abba Bessarion, one of the Egyptian desert fathers, taught that "the monk ought to be . . . all eye."[3] This powerful lesson still rings true 1,500 years later. We need to be giant, all-seeing eyeballs. Not like the evil eye of Sauron in J. R. R. Tolkien's *The Lord of the Rings,* but passionate, caring eyes that seek out the lessons that God has for us today. We need to see the lessons that are right in front of us with all their complexities and harsh realities.

Engaging the sources of theology requires action. You cannot sit back and remain passive. Remember, we *do* theology; we do not just merely *record* it. Even reading theology should not be performed passively. Theology happens all around us, whether we see it or not. Theology requires a verb-like existence of seeking, reading, searching, listening, praying, asking, struggling, wondering, probing, pushing, pulling, responding, crying, discerning.[4] Get the idea? To become a good writer of engaged theology we need to read a lot, see a lot of life, and write a lot. William Zinsser inspires me when he writes:

> to look for your material everywhere, not just by reading the obvious sources and interviewing the obvious people. Look at signs and at billboards and at all the junk written along the American roadside. Read the labels on our packages and the instructions on our toys, the claims on our medicines and the graffiti on our walls. Read the fillers, so rich in self-esteem, that come spilling out of your monthly statement from the electric company and the telephone company and the bank. Read menus and catalogues and

2. Stockton, *A Pen and a Path,* vi.

3. *Sayings of the Desert Fathers,* 42.

4. Veling, *Practical Theology,* 25

second-class mail. Nose about in obscure crannies of the newspa-per, like the Sunday real estate section—you can tell the temper of a society by what patio stories it wants. Our daily landscape is thick with absurd messages and portents. Notice them. They not only have social significance; they are often just quirky enough to make a lead that's different from everybody else's.[5]

The sources of theology dwell everywhere. But seeing and listening are hard work. The Bible, experience, tradition, and research provide great places to start engaging in theological reflection. Does theology require all four? No. Is theology stronger and deeper when all four are engaged? Yes. But you also have to learn to see what lies in front of the source, inside it, and behind it to really understand. You must be willing to be changed by what you encounter. Engaged theology isn't easy.

Seeing through Ordinary Blindness

Being a giant eyeball means more than just glancing at the source. Theo-logian Terrence Tilley provides a great example when he argues that most people when they play or listen to music don't stop to dissect the music. He writes "similarly, we will not stop to analyze an item of our experience."[6] We don't stop to think about many of the things we hear, see, taste, smell, and touch in our daily lives. We experience, whether through sight, touch, smell, taste, or hearing, tens of thousands of possible sources for theology every day. But, as in Tilley's example, though we hear the background mu-sic, we rarely try to comprehend it. Most music goes in one ear and out the other without being pulled into the higher thinking parts of our brains.

British theologian Stephen Pattison, a very good writer himself, sug-gests that many humans suffer from "ordinary blindness." He proposes that humans must consider how we perceive and relate to the world through sight. I would add our other senses as well. Ordinary blindness happens when a person physically sees something but has learned to filter it out, to become blind to it. As a result, they don't really process what they're seeing. We learn not to see what is right in front of us. We become blind to the ordinary and sometimes we become blind to the extraordinary. We learn not to see what we don't want to see—our homeless, the food on the plate before us, the ordinary, everyday things with which we come in contact. We

5. Zinsser, *On Writing Well*, 58–59.
6. Tilley, *Story Theology*, 24.

teach our brains to filter out these sights. Our eyes see. Our brain dismisses: not important, not important, not important. Pattison believes we are being held back by our "arrogant eye."[7] An arrogant eye passes over what it considers unimportant. It chooses not to see because it believes that those items don't matter.

Pattison argues for a notion of "haptic" vision. He argues, "the haptic denotes the sense of vision that touches, caresses, and interacts more mutually with objects, rather than just surveying them from afar."[8] To see objects with this haptic vision means becoming conscious of them. It means we actually think about what we are seeing. Becoming a writer of theology requires us to remove the arrogance from our eye and really see what is right in front of us. You must make both the ordinary and the extraordinary significant. You must teach your brains to engage the world around you and not filter it out. You must become conscious of the sources all around you. Seeing is the next step in becoming an engaged theologian who has the ability to recognize significant subjects.

Take a Moment to Reflect

1. Can you describe a time when you realized that you had been blind to someone or something?

2. What made you realize your blindness?

Interpreting and Discerning

Next, we need to do something with what we see. We need to discern and interpret. We need to engage meaning at many different levels. As we look at the sources of theology, we need to see more than what's on the surface. We need to examine what's underneath—root causes, long-term effects, and short-term consequences. We need to draw out what is hidden. Many theologians label this process "hermeneutics," but I like to call it interpretation. They are both long words, but thinking of this process as interpretation feels less intimidating than thinking of it as gaining hermeneutical insights. But regardless of what I think, use the term you like. Taking "seeing" to the

7. Pattison, *Seeing Things*, 19.
8. Ibid., 15.

next level is interpreting. It asks: "What does this mean?" I always connect interpretation to discernment to highlight the spiritual nature of theological interpretation.

Theologian Terry Veling presents a great analogy of eating the scroll.[9] Veling borrows this analogy from Ezekiel. In this story, God tells the prophet "O mortal, eat what is offered to you; eat this scroll, and go, speak to the house of Israel. So I opened my mouth. . . . Then I ate it; and in my mouth it was as sweet as honey."[10] Eating the scroll means digesting what we see and interpreting it. We internalize it. It becomes part of us, our reality, our being. We make something out of it. We understand it at a deeper level. Veling writes, "the reader savors the text as one who savors the fruit of the vine."[11] Interpreting requires us to digest what we see. To chew it up, savor it, swallow it, feel its texture going down our throats, and draw nourishment from it. When we engage in processes of interpretation and discernment, we unpack layers of meaning for ourselves and our audience.

These processes are very similar to archaeology. We dig down and excavate. We dig through the layers of other people's interpretation, we plow through our own embedded assumptions, and we adopt different tools to interpret what we find. Over my years of writing theology I have learned many aspects of interpretation and discernment, and there are many wonderful books you can read on these subjects, but in this chapter I want to make four points.

First, I recommend the engaged theologian bring their sources into correlation with each other. Theologians Howard Stone and James Duke define correlation as "the process of bringing two or more discrete entities into mutual relation with each other."[12] If we take experience A, mix in theologian B, and add a good dose of Scripture C, what comes out? What emerges if we mix an experience we had on the expressway during rush-hour with a dose of Scripture on Sabbath and research on burnout? When we bring sources into correlation, we create hybrid ideas that contain aspects of "A," "B," and "C." Correlation requires us to interpret one item in light of another. It brings the unlike together and troubles our minds. Anne Lamott explains that new insights "will float into your head like a goldfish, lovely, bright orange, and weightless, and you follow them like a child

9. Veling, "Listening," 208.

10. Ezekiel 3:1–3 (NRSV).

11. Veling, *Practical Theology*, xvii.

12. Stone and Duke, *How to Think Theologically*, 30.

looking at an aquarium that was thought to be without fish."[13] Correlation causes these new insights to swim into the fish bowls of our minds.

Many theologians have developed various models of correlation; I am not advocating any one particular model. I engage this term as a form of mutual correlation. I encourage writers of theology to pick an existing model or design their own. My type of correlation views the process as a conversation. Visualize the sources of theology sitting around a big conference table littered with electronic devices, papers, books, drinks, snacks, and everything else you can imagine. On the wall, there are charts and word diagrams. Ideas are being voiced across the room in one big, messy exchange of questions, possible answers, insights, jokes, illustrations, and side bars. Correlation provides a back-and-forth of questions, possible answers, and epiphanies.[14] I am not designing a theological method here, rather, engaging the sources for theology.

During the process of correlation, I suggest looking for borderlands. Gloria Anzaldúa explains that "a borderland is a dividing line, a narrow strip along a steep edge. A borderland is a vague and undetermined place created by the emotional residue of an unnatural boundary."[15] Borderlands exist when Scriptures, tradition, experience, and research rub against each other. Borderlands are dangerous places for a pilgrimage, full of unknowns, uncertainities, and dramatic questions. Many readers appear very comfortable reading Scripture, encountering tradition, studying research, or interpreting an experience in isolation. But bring three or four of these sources together and many readers enter a borderland where a reassuring author becomes a welcome friend. Borderlands are uncomfortable places that require us to construct meaning. Engaged theology needs you to cross borders and live in these borderlands.

Anzaldúa calls for "la facultad" that "is the capacity to see in surface phenomena the meaning of deeper realities, to see the deep structure below the surface. It is an instant 'sensing' a quick perception arrived at without conscious reasoning."[16] She believes that this power to sense is a breaking through that "makes us pay attention to the soul and we are thus carried into awareness—an experiencing of soul (self)."[17] Theologians need to sit

---

13. Lamott, *Bird by Bird*, 136.

14. Cameron et al., *Talking About God in Practice*, 4.

15. Anzaldúa, *Borderlands La Frontera*, 25

16. Ibid., 60.

17. Ibid., 61.

down to breakfast, look at their plates of eggs, bacon, and toast. Their plates should be jumping off points to engage in conversations on hospitality, family meals, farm worker rights, God's creation, the economics of hunger, Jesus' feeding of the hungry, the impact of corporate farming, causes of climate change, human work, agriculture, domestic life, cooking, etc., and bring these everyday experiences into dialogue with Scripture, research, and tradition. You need to discern much more than the plate of bacon and eggs; you need to take your readers into these borderlands.

As you move deeper into interpretation and discernment, you need to realize that different eyes look on the same item or moment and see different realties. The view from the pulpit and the pew are vastly different. Interpretation and discernment should never be done in isolation. Ask other people what they see. Look for other insights, engage people with radically different backgrounds and perspectives, and listen—really listen. What are they saying? Why are they saying this? Dig deep. You need to let other voices rock your foundations.

Never let this discernment become unhooked from theological interpretation. Take time, make space, push away the distractions and interruptions of other people, and listen for the voice of God. God doesn't speak to one person alone. I suggest jumping back and re-reading the section on discernment in chapter 2.

We should use our writing process to help us interpret and discern. Anzaldúa explains, "that's what writing is for me, an endless cycle of making it worse, making it better, but always making meaning out of the experience whatever it may be."[18] We need to write into our ideas. Writing provides a process of thinking. As we record our thoughts onto screen or notebook, we give ourselves the opportunity to add layers of interpretation to what we are thinking, to re-organize our thoughts, and to add dimensions through correlation.

TAKE A MOMENT TO REFLECT

1. What borders have been difficult for you to cross? Why?

18. Ibid., 95.

Reading Scripture

Scripture provides the first major source for theology. Engaged theology requires Scripture. Scripture gives the breath of the spirit within theology. As a source for theology, Scripture contains both a spiritual element and a scholarly element. Theologians Howard Stone and James Duke believe "the significance of the Bible for theology, however, cannot be reduced to its value as a historical record."[19] Rather, the spiritual element and the scholarly element both need to be present within an engaged theology.

But dangers exist here. Quoting a lot of Scripture doesn't make words theology. We must avoid both eisegesis and proof-texting. Stone and Duke define eisegesis as "a derogatory term for the practice of imposing one's own ideas on Scripture rather than drawing out the meaning of the text by careful, thoroughgoing study."[20] They then define proof-texting as "the practice of picking and choosing portions of the Scripture to support a particular (pre-chosen) view."[21] Both of these practices must be avoided at all cost. Be fearful of convenient interpretations and guard against overly individualistic insights.

As a spiritual element, Scripture should nurture spiritual growth. As theologian Kathleen Norris observes, "daily meditation on Scripture in which one reads not for knowledge or information but to enhance one's life of faith."[22] Engaging with Scripture should nourish your spiritual growth and reading Scripture in your work should stimulate your readers' spiritual growth. Scripture should be as natural as breathing. Engagement with Scripture should bring writers and readers into a closer relationship with each other and with God. Possible passages should leap out of memories and into our texts. But just because Scripture should have a spiritual element, it does not mean Scripture should never be unsettling or upsetting.

Theologian Debbie Blue believes "people may have been reading it [Scripture] carefully for thousands of years but this doesn't mean something new might not walk out of it."[23] If the Bible is not blowing our minds and troubling our thoughts, maybe we need to go back and read it again and again. We also need to study how previous generations understood

---

19. Stone and Duke, *How to Think Theologically,* 47.

20. Ibid., 134.

21. Ibid., 136.

22. Norris, *Amazing Grace,* 277.

23. Blue, *Consider the Birds,* 74.

the passages we engage. Each and every generation added new layers of interpretation to Scripture. These interpretations provide doorways through which to engage the scholarly element of Scripture as well as serving as windows for viewing the spirituality reflected by our theological parents. But they may also be roadblocks that you need to tear down to hear the authentic message for today.

The scholarly element of Scripture requires us, the interpreters, to get behind the text, to get within the text, and to get in front of the text. The Bible is a culturally distanced book. A lot has changed since Jesus walked the dusty roads of Galilee, and even more has changed since earliest passages of the Genesis were first written onto a scroll. And even more has changed since the first oral stories were told around a camp fire. Getting behind the text opens layers of meaning that we miss with our modern eyes.

Getting behind the text requires us to study and attempt to understand how the original audience heard those words. Some of the doorways behind the text include linguistic studies, social-historical studies, source and authorship studies, and cultural studies. Getting within the text allows us to engage the story itself: the genre, the characters, the plot, the diction, and many other aspects of the passage. Getting in front of the text encourages us to examine the Scripture in light of the present, and open ourselves to understanding how other interpreters have examined it in light of their own times.

But even the scholarly aspects of scriptural study come through the eyes of the believer for the theologian. As theologian Richard Lischer explains "the consumerist shines a flashlight on the text and says, 'tell me all you know.' The religious reader allows the light of the text to illumine his or her own life and that of the congregation."[24] We must not be consumers of Scriptures but people willing to be illuminated by Scripture from behind, within, and in front of the text. Each doorway and window behind these scholarly processes deepens our understanding of the passage and its correlation to our other sources.

Take a Moment to Reflect

1. What is the hardest aspect of writing about the Bible for you? Why?

24. Lischer, *The End of Words*, 68.

Reading Tradition

As a theologian who grew up in an evangelical tradition, attended an evangelical university as an undergrad, earned a Master of Divinity from an ecumenical seminary with a majority of progressive Protestants, and graduated with a PhD in practical theology from a Roman Catholic University, my appreciation for tradition has grown over the years. Never believe that engaged theology requires anyone to adopt a mindset of Scripture versus tradition. Our readings of Scripture and tradition should edify each other. Tradition gives writers of theology a rich source to mine.

I really began to understand tradition at a much deeper level after reading an illustration that Richard Osmer, a Presbyterian theologian, presents in the preface to one of his books. The illustration comes from John of Salisbury, who attributes it to Bernard of Chartres, so it's been around for a while. It goes like this: "we are like dwarfs on the shoulders of giants, so that we can see more than they, and things at a greater distance, not by virtue of any sharpness on our part, or any physical distinction, but because we are carried high and raised up by their giant size."[25] We can only do the theology we do today because of the men and women who came before us. We are not smarter than them. We only see farther because we are standing on the backs of their work. Tradition is simply the transmission of Christianity across generations and across cultural boundaries. Tradition shows up in the stories and actions of our faith.

Roman Catholic theologian Yves Congar argues that "tradition is memory, and memory enriches experiences. If we remember nothing it would be impossible to advance. . . . True tradition is not servility but fidelity."[26] He compares tradition to a "relay race, where the runners, spaced at intervals, pass an object from one to the other, a baton, for example, or a torch."[27] While another Roman Catholic theologian, Terry Veling, explains tradition as a gift; he writes, "we sometimes think of tradition as tired and worn, old and dusty, but it is first and foremost a *gift*. Among other things, it is the gift of memory—a memory that is older and larger than my life."[28] Methodist theologian William Willimon uses a story to explain tradition. He writes,

25. Osmer, *Practical Theology*, viii.

26. Congar, *The Meaning of Tradition*, 8.

27. Ibid., 14–15.

28. Veling, *Practical Theology*, 34

when I walk with Jesus, a considerable crowd of unlikely saints walk with me, giving me encouragement for the journey, an invitation to join in a conversation which began long before we were born and shall continue long after we are dead—God rendered through literature, ancient and modern, God with us as the Word made flesh, then made words so that we might be the World enfleshed again.[29]

Willimon believes that "no Christian prays or believes or acts alone. . . . We are formed by the saints—those who came before us."[30] The majority of the transmission of tradition takes place in the ordinary lived daily life of the faith. Watching a grandmother pray. Seeing people being baptized on Easter. Tradition embodies rites, behaviors, and objects that anchor us in our faith. Tradition is history, but it is also more than that. History is never just telling it like it is; it is always under interpretation because everyone writes within the social context of their own embedded theology, as well as with a purpose. We must always remember that tradition is never free from baggage just as our writing will never be free from baggage. As we read these descriptions of tradition, we can understand that tradition has many different meanings. And I believe we must always add an "s" to it. Tradition must be understood as traditions. There is never just one tradition. Christianity embodies many traditions. Tradition remains a plural noun even when we don't add the letter "s." We can't forget this. These traditions are our past and our present. Traditions are our inherited stories and actions. But traditions are also being birthed today in the present. Our legacy to those yet to come.

So what do writers of theology need to know about engaging traditions as a source of theology? I feel that when we bring our theological narratives into correlation with traditions, we enter into an ongoing conversation. We make ourselves one of the voices. We are never the voice of tradition, but one of its conversation partners. These conversations started long before we were born and they will continue long after we are food for worms. Traditions are a dialogue both forward and backward. Traditions give us our roots, our foundations, as well as our building plans for tomorrow.

But theologians must never confuse tradition with traditionalism. Traditionalism is a graveyard of beliefs and actions done without thought or living faith. Traditionalism consists of performing an action as it has

29. Willimon, *Reading with Deeper Eyes*, 14.
30. Ibid., 11.

been done before just because that is how it has always been done. Traditionalism exists as a symptom of death, while tradition embodies healthy development. As we write theology, we must engage tradition but not traditionalism.

Tradition equips us with a powerful tool against traditionalism. German theologian Johannes Baptist Metz points out the power of dangerous memories. He writes, "there is another way to remember: dangerous memories, memories that challenge."[31] As writers, when we claim dangerous memories, we can challenge traditionalism. We can break the cycles of unhealthy repetitious behaviors. Dangerous memories exist through the width and breadth of tradition. These memories come from many different stories. Metz observes that "this means a dangerous memory not just of those who have emerged the victors, but rather of those who collapsed along the way."[32] As new experiences and new problems rub against tradition, theologians will gain new insights and voice new possibilities for being Christian.

Kathleen Norris illustrates another reality of tradition. She explains, "human inheritance is both blessing and curse. And in religious inheritance this paradox is acute. For many of us religion is heavy baggage. Stories of love and fear, liberation and constriction, grace and malice come not only from our own experiences, and our family's past, but from an ancestral history within a tradition."[33] We must engage tradition and stories between the lines. Tradition handed down in the public and official narratives of the church are never the full record. Engaged theology must provide a tradition with surpluses of meaning. Tradition develops into a curse for theology when it is exclusive to the story of Christianity in Europe, or turns into "shorthand for hegemonic theology."[34] When writers remake tradition into their own images, great evils can be inflicted upon the faith.

Each and every element of tradition must be interpreted. As we unpack tradition, we need to look for the suppressed stories. For the losers whose stories were silenced and censored. Theologian James Cochrane notes, "each and every element of it must be understood as situationally bound, revealing and concealing simultaneously. No complete truth may be found here, at least not by human beings. Even the most cherished

---

31. Metz, *Faith in History and Society*, 105.

32. Ibid., 208.

33. Norris, *Amazing Grace*, 22.

34. Macy, "The Iberian Heritage of US Latino/a Theology," 47.

confessions and creeds are bound in this way."[35] We need to seek what has been concealed. We might never find the whole truth but we can expose more truths. Breaking down barriers created by racism, sexism, classism, nationalism, to name a few, allows for a more engaged theology.

On the positive side, tradition roots us. Tradition gives writers of theology so many resources. The sources are rich and deep, especially as we develop our ability to read between the lines. Living traditions are growing traditions. They tie us to our pasts. They help form our identity. I live in a hurricane zone. Roots are important here. They help us stand in the face of life's storms. They allow us to draw nourishment from the soil, to grow stronger and taller and reach out. Roots both anchor and nourish us.

During the storms, tradition anchors our theology. Howard Stone and James Duke explain, "one way to guard against getting caught up in the implicit theology of the present culture, or being blown along by the latest wind of doctrine, is to take seriously the resources of tradition."[36] Pop culture and the latest fads tend to blow into churches. Sometimes this is great, but sometimes it has horrible consequences. When the newest trend empowers the faithful to reach out and grow closer to God and each other, it's great. When the newest fad reduces the church to a business, a charity, or delivers it into the hands of a political party or government, then it's bad. Very bad. Tradition provides many examples of this, both good and bad. Theologians engage tradition to help us guard against these negative forces.

Tradition gives hope and hope sustains the soul. Poet John Leax highlights this hope. He notes "I needed to hear extensive testimony from those who have gone before me about the struggles, trials and rewards of the vocation of writing."[37] The stories of tradition let us hear from those who have walked the roads of faith. These are our ancestors. They faced struggles that parallel many of our own. Our Mothers and Fathers of the faith give us role models. They give us stories about how to live faith, stories that illustrate the mistakes Christianity has made in the past. Their stories give us hope.

As writers of engaged theology, we recall, we reinvent, we remodel the sources of traditions to empower believers to contend with new questions that arise from daily life. We bring it into correlation with new experiences, changing situations, and bring our readers to a richer, deeper engaged theology.

35. Cochrane, *Circles of Dignity*, 47.
36. Stone and Duke, *How to Think Theologically*, 50.
37. Leax, *Grace is Where I Live*, 15.

Reading Experience

"Experience," our next source for theology, is a broad umbrella term that covers many concepts. Like the concepts of Scripture and tradition in the preceding sections, whole books have been composed about theologically interpreting experience. And engaged theology thirsts for experiences. In these few pages, I want to touch upon three sources of experiences: ourselves, culture, and other people. Humans learn by experience. Our first reaction when we encounter something new is to relate it to our past experiences to understand it better. Experiences are powerful. They can go off like a bomb in our minds. From the unique, once-in-a-lifetime experience to a childhood memory that evokes a powerful response, experiences keep giving.

For novelist E. L. Doctorow the experience of reading two words, "Loon Lake," on a road sign gave birth to three-hundred pages.[38] Now that's an experience that goes off like a bomb in one's mind. Think of the world as a text waiting to be read, or as a garage sale where someone else's junk becomes your treasure. Author Anne Lamott provides the following example: "life is like a recycling center, where all the concerns and dramas of humankind get recycled back and forth across the universe. But what you have to offer is your own sensibility, maybe your own sense of humor or inside pathos or meaning. All of us can sing the same song, and there will still be four billion different renditions."[39] You need to become a witness to experience, as I suggested earlier, not just seeing it but comprehending it. Engaged theology requires experiences.

All the experiences that you use as sources for theology begin with you—the theologian. You begin with your interpretation of these experiences. You read yourself. Your life is a dense, multidimensional, layered,

---

38. Lehmann-Haupt, "Books of the Times."
39. Lamott, *Bird by Bird*, 181.

complex weave of responses: emotional, intellectual, physical, and spiritual. You sense experiences both through your physical senses and other ways of knowing. And to make lived experience even more complex, you don't experience experiences in isolation, you exist in relationship with God and others in a time and place.

The process of reading ourselves begins with reflection. You start with your own experiences and try to figure out what they mean theologically. Peruvian theologian, Gustavo Gutiérrez, explains that "this is what Bernard of Clairvaux put so beautifully when he said that when it comes to spirituality all people must know how to 'drink from their own wells.'"[40] As theological writers you must learn how to drink from the wells of your own experiences. The key aspect here is learning. We must learn how to use these life-giving waters to nourish ourselves and others, and bring ourselves and them into closer relationship with God. Learning these skills is very difficult.

The vital source that we as theologians need to read is ourselves, our experiences, our lives. If you survived your childhood and teenage years, you probably have enough source material to write for a lifetime. Ron Klug engages the dramatic verb "harvests" to explain to authors what they need to do with their own spiritual autobiographies.[41] As theologians harvest the fruits of their personal experiences, they need to bring these experiences into conversation with research, tradition, and Scripture to take their theological expression to the next level.

A significant aspect of reading yourself and your experiences is recognizing that you are not alone. We are who we are because of others. Theologian Laurie Green makes this really simple when he engages an African proverb: "A person is a person because of other people."[42] We exist as theologians and as people in a web of relationships that form and shape us into our past selves, our present selves, and our future selves. But as you reflect on these webs of relations, you also must reflect on the time and space in which these relationships occur. You live in the world. Luci Shaw illustrates this when she writes, "crisis times—widowhood, divorce, suicide, job loss, ill health, broken relationships—can become the defining and refining moments of our lives, and unless we achieve a kind of deep honesty with ourselves as flawed, broken people, I'm not sure that we can write with the

40. Gutiérrez, *We Drink From Our Own Wells*, 5.

41. Klug, *How to Keep a Spiritual Journal*, 121.

42. Green, *Let's Do Theology*, 10.

authenticity that will reach other people where they need to be reached."[43] Engaging your own experiences as a source for theology requires you to dig deep, exploring the dark closets where theology hides.

Often, engaged experiences begin to hurt when you become honest about them. You can't write engaged theology if you write about how you think you should feel or how you want to feel; rather, you must record how you really feel. You might think, as you trust in a living God, that you should write that you are resting in the arms of God even during a crisis, when in fact you are falling into a bottomless pit of hopeless despair. Engaged theology expresses how you feel, not how you want to feel.

The value of experience as a source is confined only by the narrowness of our own experiences. As Anne Lamott explains, "one of the gifts of being a writer is that it gives you an excuse to do things, to go places and explore. Another is that writing motivates you to look closely at life, at life as it lurches by and tramps around."[44] This is the paradoxical reality of being a writer; we need to go out and experience as much of life as we can so that we can sit in small rooms and write about it. If we learn to pay attention, each event offers us a multitude of meanings. No event is un-interpreted and every event has multiple meanings.

Experience as a source for theology encompasses both our personal experiences and our experiences of the wider culture. Ordinary acts like eating, shopping, cleaning, driving, and working become realities with which to grasp the ultimate principles if we reflect on them with the help of Scripture, tradition, and research. Everything is both ordinary and extraordinary. Write about the ordinary; the extraordinary often blooms from it.

As you expand your circle of personal experiences, you encounter the wider experiences of culture. Every time you switch on your television, use an app on your phone, or walk down the street, you encounter culture. Culture is all around us. It exists embedded in each and every interaction we have. It is in your entertainment, your food, your social interactions. And wider cultural experiences burst with potential for theology. Wider cultural experiences emerge as the cutting edge of theological reflection. It is where people looking for answers and insights. Culture remains a prime subject for crafting theology. The cultural sources for theology are nearly endless: movies, music, art, architecture, advertising, protests, economic statistics, and on and on. Engage them.

43. Shaw, "The Writer's Notebook," 24.
44. Lamott, *Bird by Bird*, xii.

As we delve into our experiences, begin by crafting detailed descriptions of these moments. Replay them again and again. Reflect on each and every aspect. We need to use our writing to think, to pour out our memories, layer upon layer upon layer, crafting rich, deep descriptions. Read and re-read these descriptions and ask yourself, what do I find the most interesting? What experience is calling to me? This is the entry point. This is where you go deeper. Explore this aspect on paper. Trust that the heart of the message will emerge as you write. Let this message grow. Bring it into encounter with Scripture, tradition, and research. Let the idea flourish and mature.

While writing about experiences, you should always look for ways to improve your presentation and reflection. First, I recommend that you let experiences age. Like cheese and wine, experience matures with age. The experience doesn't change but your perception of it may. An important experience will not diminish with time. In fact, your ability to remember it might actually improve. Secondly, look for the story within the story. Many of your experiences are so layered and multidimensional that you can't examine every detail without overwhelming your readers. One element from the entire experience might be enough to engage. Finally, dive into the deep end and don't waste your time wading in the kiddy pool. Bring the experience into conversation. Use Scripture, tradition, and research to interpret it. Read it, fight with it. Build your words into action.

Finally, another wonderful source of experience is other people. We encounter their stories on television and social media, in books, and most importantly in conversation with our families, friends, and total strangers. Make sure to have permission to write about their experience. Even when writing about another's experience, we do it through our own lens as we retell. It is a great gift to be entrusted to tell someone else's story. Telling someone's story requires us to listen, *truly listen*. Often when people talk, we are only half listening. We spend most of the time thinking about how we are going to reply. We must give people our full attention. We must watch, listen, and seek the theology that happens between people. Relationships overflow with theological potential.

When we write profiles and biographies, we tell stories on other people's experience. We interpret their faith, their experiences, and their behaviors to empower our readers' faith lives. We become carriers of tradition. We re-tell their stories not to make them saints but to capture their faith as humanly as possible. No one is perfect. And no matter how much we come to admire and love our subjects, we need to explore their victories and their failures in our stories. We have a responsibility to our readers and a duty to our subjects.

Engaged theology requires the source of experience.

Take a Moment to Reflect

1. Is there one experience in your life that you have always wanted to write about?
2. If so, what is stopping you from writing about it?

Reading Research

The final source guide we need to read for our journey is research. Research empowers us to interpret experience, Scripture, and tradition. Anne Lamott explains:

> Books help us understand who we are and how we are to behave. They show us what community and friendship mean; they show us how to live and die. They are full of all the things that you don't get in real life—wonderful, lyrical language, for instance, right off the bat. And quality of attention: we may notice amazing details during the course of a day but we rarely let ourselves stop and really pay attention. An author makes you notice, makes you pay attention, and this is a great gift. My gratitude for good writing is unbounded; I'm grateful for it the way I'm grateful for the ocean. Aren't you? I ask.[45]

I love research. It's like a treasure hunt. I never know what I'll find or where I'll find it. Research appears in many forms and mediums: print materials, interviews with people, original research methodologies. We can do research by searching in libraries, walking down the street, watching our televisions, surfing the net, going to the theatre, reading advertisements at a local coffee shop, asking other people . . .

As a theological librarian, my research always begins with books and articles. But there exist other places to begin research. Novelist Stephen King argues, "every book you pick up has its own lesson or lessons, and

---

45. Ibid., 15.

quite often the bad books have more to teach you than the good ones."[46] Everything we read has a lesson for us even if the lesson is "don't do it this way." The more we read the less likely we are to write something dumb and empty. We need to learn our sources and engage them. We need to build a deep understanding of the research on our subjects, even the sources we disagree with. Liberals need to read conservative materials and conservatives need to read liberal materials. And both need to read with an open mind. I don't care whether you start with books or by developing an original research methodology. Pick a place and start digging. Learn all you can, write all you can, and share all you can.

Research is as essential to theology as water is for life. As Natalie Goldberg writes, "we never expect to drink a glass of water just once in our lives. A book can be that essential too."[47] We must return again and again to our research partners, including partners who are not theologians. Multidisciplinary engagement not only supports engaged theology, it is necessary for an engaged theology.

TAKE A MOMENT TO REFLECT

1. Describe your most vivid memory of a library.
2. What is your least favorite part of research? Why?

Conclusion

You might have noticed that as I went through this second chapter on engaged theology I didn't mention methodology. My reason is that there are so many wonderful books, articles, and guides on doing theology. My simple unpacking of correlation in this chapter does not represent my theological methodology. I only highlight it to remind us all that sources of theology need to provoke each of us in order to give us insights. At the end of the book, you will find a bibliography of some of my favorite titles. I suggest we all keep reading. Before we end this chapter on engaged theology and move on to the concept of compelling theology, I want to conclude by suggesting

46. King, *On Writing*, 145.
47. Goldberg, *Thunder and Lightning*, 115.

that we always need to return to our sources and ask ourselves, what makes this theological? Never stray from this.

Engaged theology needs the sources of Scripture, tradition, experience, and research. Insights into theological engagement grow daily and our knowledge needs to keep up. Good luck!

PS: After all my complaining at the beginning of this chapter, I wrote my first draft in three days. This was a lesson to me that when I engage my sources before writing, the writing flows naturally.

An Epistle to Graduate Students

Dear Sisters and Brothers,

Pilgrimages should not be easy. The study of theology is not for wimps and lazy souls, or lazy people in general. Theology means sweat. If you want to do something easy with your life, the graduate study of theology isn't it. Expect to be challenged; and if you aren't challenged, go somewhere else to study. Being challenged isn't just about being forced to work hard; rather, being challenged includes being forced to think in new ways, ways that may leave you unsure or uncomfortable.

I encourage you to take this jump seriously and faithfully. You are never too young or too old to begin graduate theological studies. I had a great friend who started her master's degree at age seventy, graduated at age seventy-five, and worked as a chaplain at a children's hospital well into her eighties. I have also met great, engaged writers barely out of their teen years. Theology is an activity of transformation, and transformation is a process, not a one-time event. Engage, explore, and ask questions.

Look for ways to challenge yourself as a writer. Austin Kleon notes "Dr. Seuss wrote *The Cat in the Hat* with only 236 different words, so his editor bet him he couldn't write a book with only 50 different words. Dr. Seuss came back and won the bet with *Green Eggs and Ham*, one of the bestselling children's books of all time."[1] Now that is a challenge. Push and pull yourself to the limits of the English language.

Outgrow poor writing habits that you formed in high school and college. Many young writers believe the purpose of research is to take several sources and summarize them. Author A believes this, author B argues for this, and author C recommends this. Add an introduction and a conclusion that summarizes all three major points and you have a research paper. Right? Wrong! This is false research. Real research writing

1. Kleon, *Steal Like an Artist*, 138.

develops around a burning question that doesn't have a simple answer, compares and contrasts what major sources argue, and forms original conclusions and insights. Add to the conservation. Don't bore your readers with the same old arguments and ideas; give them something fresh.

If you run out of ideas, make your brain uncomfortable. Kleon argues that when "your brain gets too comfortable in your everyday surroundings, you need to make it uncomfortable. You need to spend some time in another land, among people that do things differently than you. Travel makes the world look new, and when the world looks new, our brains work harder."[2] Engage experiences, both ordinary and extraordinary ones. A walk about the block while you are truly paying attention can be just as extraordinary as a trip around the world. Pay attention, open your eyes and see the world past the surface. Exercise your imagination daily. Work it out!

Read, write, and experience everything you can. I love this passage that Austin Kleon borrows from Jim Jarmusch (even if he didn't cite the publication),

> Steal from anywhere that resonates with inspiration or fuels your imagination. Devour old films, new films, music, books, paintings, photographs, poems, dreams, random conversations, architecture, bridges, street signs, trees, clouds, bodies of water, light and shadows. Select only things to steal from that speak directly to your soul. If you do this, your work (and theft) will be authentic.[3]

But your reading needs to go deeper than it did when you were an undergraduate. Find a thinker who sets your brain on fire and delve deep. Read everything they have ever written. Study how they write. Look at their sources. Discover what they loved and hated. Find the authors they love and read them too. Who inspired your thinker? Who are their muses? Who inspired your thinker's role models? Learn everything about them. Trace their intellectual pedigree. Find the cutting edges. Discover the borderlands where mainline thinkers fear to go. And chase down every citation to build upon the edges of theological knowledge. Now, unpack where you fit into this pedigree.

My friend and fellow theologian, Jonathan Best, suggested when he read an earlier draft of this epistle that I should remind you not to forget where you came from. He reminds you that you've come to the graduate study of theology with a history, a background, a set of experiences. Don't

2. Ibid., 94.
3. Ibid., 14.

forget these. You don't need to throw all this away. You might have been a lawyer, a nurse, a trash collector, a business owner whose business went belly-up. You might love video gaming or reading Russian novels. In other words, you are not a blank page when you start this pilgrimage. Don't start over; build upon what you are (your personal experiences). You don't need to become someone new for theology. Be yourself. This background is not baggage; these are the gold coins you bring to theology.

As writers of theology, start bending the rules. Work with your faculty to foster better modes of expression for your theological prose. If you've mastered the English sentence, demonstrate this to your professors and get their blessing to push the boundaries of theological communication. I recommend you start writing for the ears and eyes of your intended audience by looking at and listening to your work. How does your work look on the page? How does it sound when you read it out loud? Will it compel readers? When you hear yourself dropping into term paper mode, stop. Learn to discover what makes prose engaged, compelling, and beautiful to you. Then master what makes prose engaged, compelling, and beautiful to your intended audience.

But remember: *keep your feet on the ground*

four

Compelling Theology: Your Audience

Writing compelling theology requires that authors successfully grab their audiences' attention. One evening I was sorting books at the Biersdorf Library of Ecumenical Theological Seminary, which dwells in the basement of the old First Presbyterian Church, built in 1889, in Detroit, Michigan when an older, well-dressed man of Indian descent came into the library.

"Excuse me. Are you a Christian?" he asked.

Many conversations have strange beginnings when you're working the reference desk of a theology library. Some lead somewhere interesting. Others just get weird. So I replied, "Yes. Can I help you?"

The man smiled at me warmly and asked, "I have always wondered something. You Christians say you are monotheists. But you are really polytheists right?" It was evident—he really wanted to know.

"No, we are monotheists," I answered.

"Now, I am Hindu," he said. "I know about having a lot of gods. But you Christians have three. Right? God, Jesus, and the Spirit?"

"Yes." I nodded. "God the creator, Jesus, and the Holy Spirit are all God."

"So you are really polytheists. You have three gods."

"No, we are monotheists," I insisted. "We have one God who is God the creator, God Jesus, and God the Holy Spirit."

This went on for the next hour, and we had a wonderful conversation, but in the end he confessed, "I still don't understand." But he wanted to keep talking. And we were both enjoying our conversation.

All the stories, metaphors, and illustrations I used failed to explain to my new friend the complex realities of the Trinity. I failed my audience. Or did I?

Audience

Each of us, when we speak or write, has an audience even if it is only ourselves. If we want to write compelling theology, we need to consider our audience. Compelling theology reaches out and grabs its audience. It compels them to come back again and again. Compelling theology doesn't exist apart from engaged theology or beautiful theology; rather, it works with these other concepts to create a memorable reading experience that compels its audience to read more, to think, to act.

Being authors of theology doesn't mean only writing what we think our audiences want. We are not just putting words on the page to please adoring fans. We are not just churning out the same old story to sell books. We should seek to entertain and engage, but we need to do more than that. Compelling theology means more than getting our fans to jump on Amazon and pre-order our next book. Compelling theology is a five-star eating experience that looks good, tastes great, nourishes, and brings you back for more.

This chapter explores many of the dos and don'ts for creating a five-star dining experience for your readers. Throughout the life of your publications, your words will have many audiences (hopefully). As with any restaurant experience, some guests are expected and others just wander in off the street. We plan for our guests and open ourselves up for those who are unexpected by thinking about audience.

Intended Audience

Rule One: know your intended audience. Welcome unintended readers who show up, but focus on your intended audience first. As Constance Hale argues, "prose is an intimate exchange between the writer and reader. Always think about your reader; hold your audience in mind."[1] Plan for them. Prepare for them. You're throwing a party for them. These are your guests of honor. They are the readers you want to come to your reading party. You wouldn't serve shrimp if you knew your guest of honor had a seafood allergy. A good host plans to the last minuscule detail.

This plan begins with trust. Our readers must trust us as theologians and writers. Theologian Richard Lischer observes that "children want to read with someone who has already been through the material, who is

1. Hale, *Sin and Syntax*, 7.

thoroughly acquainted with every surprising twist in the story and who can guarantee its ending for them. They want to read with someone they trust."[2] This is true for all readers, not just children. Would you read a book by an author you couldn't trust? Would you quote an author in a sermon or an article if you weren't sure they were trustworthy? Our readers need to trust us. We must prove our words to be reliable, trustworthy, and accurate. This means we can't take shortcuts in doing our research. We can't skip steps in the writing process. We must check and double-check. Don't give your readers any reason to not trust your words. Trust is the foundation of a great relationship between reader and author.

You hold the burden of empowering the reader to trust and understand you. This compels readers to return, to read deeper, and to explore your ideas. Joseph McCormack believes "only an arrogant author would expect you to read the book cover to cover to figure out what he's trying to say."[3] Authors cannot afford to be arrogant. When readers sense arrogance, their distrust grows. You must approach your readers with humility and thanksgiving. You are host, guide, and protector as they journey through your words.

You also have to understand what motivates your readers. Why will people want or need to read what you write? You need to understand what motivates your readers to delve into your words. You need to explore their needs and wants. Joseph McCormack argues that you must "know what motivates your audience. If you miss this part, you run the risk of losing people—and their attention, respect, time, or trust—right from the start."[4] We, as writers of theology, need to discern why people will want to read our words. Again, why will people want or need to read what you write?

The answer to this "why" question affects everything. It impacts your style, language, illustrations, the use of Scripture, the length of your work, how you edit and revise, and on and on. When you know who your intended audience is and what motivates them to read your work, you know what is appropriate for them. You wouldn't use a lot of farming illustrations if your intended audience consists of young adults growing up in an urban environment. You wouldn't write in a hip-hop style if your intended audience is made up of retired baby-boomers living in the suburbs. You

---

2. Lischer, *The End of Words*, 67.

3. McCormack, *Brief*, 101.

4. Ibid., 160.

wouldn't use informal, slang language if your intended audience is made up of college professors. Always plan for your intended audience.

As an author, you need to understand your intended audience's worldview. Richard Lischer explains, "what we actually have is a series of filters superimposed upon one another, which includes but is not limited to our experience, context, race, gender, class, and most of all, our convictions about how God is present to us in the world—our theology. No hermeneutic can do away with these very human filters without doing away with the humanity of the reader as well."[5] In chapter 2, I asked you to consider your embedded theology. Now, I am reminding you to understand your audiences' embedded theology. Never write simply what you think they want.[6] Know when you are shaking your readers from the familiarity of their comfort zones. Know when you're pushing them. Know when you're challenging their preconceived beliefs. Hopefully, you have already established a sense of trust, now you have to move them from where they are to where you want them to go.

Moving your audience requires hospitality. You need to know whether to greet your readers with a hardy handshake, a hug and kiss on the cheek, or a passionate embrace. But we must begin by greeting them, making them feel welcome. Often in theology, we call on people to change and feel like yelling "Look at yourselves, you idiots!" Instead, we need to gently encourage them to realize: "This is who we are."[7] It is about hospitality. We need to offer them a drink, not grab them by the neck and pour it down their throats. Christianity, like most religions, political parties, and worldviews shows its worst side when it becomes defensive.[8] When readers feel unwelcome, they stop reading. When they feel confused, they stop reading. When they see a butterfly, they stop reading. Our hospitality keeps compelling them back to the text.

5. Lischer, *The End of Words*, 64.

6. Norris, *Amazing Grace*, 202.

7. Lamott, *Bird by Bird*, 234.

8. Norris, *Amazing Grace*, 222.

Do No Harm

Put this on your computer screen: "Theologian, do no harm." Hospitality starts here. Doing no harm requires writers to offer "a" narrative not "the" narrative. We cannot write as *the* voice; rather, we need to offer *a* voice, an insight, a vision. Theologian Gustavo Gutierrez makes this very clear when he argues for offering "*a*, not *the*, way of being Christian."[9] Compelling theology does not harm its readers. It may challenge them. It might push and pull them. It could even exert a little spiritual pressure. But this is done in a fellowship of love.

Words hurt. Nearly every week, I come across men and women who have been spiritually crippled or emotionally maimed by a theologian's words. They bear the scars of theologians whose use of guilt, shame, and spiritual violence leave them unable to walk into a church or pray without pain. When people write out of a place of arrogance and they remake readers in their own image, readers can be devastated.

If a reader doesn't believe as you believe, leave space in your prose for them to process your ideas. Don't demand that they believe as you believe; be inclusive not exclusive. This means making little changes, like considering each and every use of the pronouns "we" and "us." A phrase like "us Christians" followed by a statement on belief will leave a Christian who believes differently feeling kicked-out and unwelcome. Theologian Kathleen Norris waves a warning flag at faith that "always wants to separate 'us' from 'them,' basing one's own security and sanctity on the fact that others may be adjudged to be deficient or impure."[10] "Us" versus "them" scenarios are rooted in harmful violence. They hurt readers. They harm fellow Christians. They drive people from the faith. An "I" statement, or a "some Christians"

9. Gutiérrez, *We Drink From Our Own Wells*, 53.

10. Norris, *Amazing Grace*, 219.

statement, creates room for readers to disagree and keep reading. Always leave your readers with a sense of hope and empowerment.

1. Have you seen harm caused by religion or theology? Examples?

Respect Your Readers

Hospitality does not end with welcoming readers and trying not to harm them. It continues with respect. Theologians must respect their readers. Our writing style and tone reflect this respect. You must build a positive relationship with your readers, one that begins with your approach. Theology requires a humble approach, not an in-your-face screaming match. Theologian Judson Edwards writes,

> The problem with the sidewalk evangelist's approach to communication is what it does to the person receiving it. If we write with that kind of in-your-face style, we assault the reader's privacy, intelligence, and goodness. Though our words might be true and biblical, our music is discordant and harsh. In our kind of world, the only thunder that has a chance of being heard is a quiet thunder that makes the listener lean forward in curiosity. Was that really thunder? Did I just catch a whiff of something truthful? Is there discovery in the air? I would propose that all of us who write adopt a style of gentle thunder that respects our readers.[11]

Don't lecture your audience; join with them to explore. When prose oozes a know-it-all, better-than-you, shut-up-and-listen-to-me, put-down attitude, readers stop reading. People don't like to be told how to think. They don't like to be lectured. People, and readers, enjoy sitting down with a friend and chatting.

We must stress that we are fellow pilgrims. We walk with our readers; we don't lead them, but walk side-by-side as fellow travelers. As you earn their trust, you must earn their friendship. Your prose must demonstrate your curiosity, your faith, and your willingness to engage them as sisters

11. Edwards, *Blissful Affliction*, 44.

and brothers. Edgar Schein argues for a process of humble inquiry, which he defines as "the fine art of drawing someone out, of asking questions to which you do not already know the answer, of building a relationship based on curiosity and interest in the other person."[12] When we understand our writing as a gift for others, a gift that we expect nothing in return for, we are on the right track. We can show readers that we are interested in helping our world, our fellow travelers, and them.

I love the image of leaving a trail of gold coins for readers. Writing expert Roy Peter Clark suggests "imagine you are walking on a narrow path through a deep forest. You stroll a mile, and there at your feet is a gold coin. You pick it up and put it in your pocket. You walk another mile, and, sure enough, you see another gold coin. What will you do next? You walk another mile in search of another coin, of course."[13] Gold coins are the gifts writers leave for readers to find. Readers will keep reading if they discover something useful, whether it is practical or entertaining. What are you leaving for your readers to find? Practical help? Emotional support? Spiritual growth? Solidarity? As you write, you need to consider what you are leaving your friends.

Our writing must demonstrate our openness to other possibilities. We cannot pretend we have all the answers. Faith remains a mystery even for spiritual gurus. Often we are asking our readers to unlearn some prior perspective. It is not easy to ask someone to alter anything they already believe. Learning something new is easy, unless readers need to unlearn something first. That is hard. Unlearning is even harder when they need to acknowledge something they knew was wrong or incomplete.[14] Edgar Schein argues, "we live in a pragmatic, problem-solving culture in which knowing things and telling others what we know is valued."[15] Like some teenagers, readers will rebel when we tell them to do something. Instead, we need to ask, suggest, and gently move them towards new possibilities. Theologians need to respect their readers. To write compelling theology requires respect. When readers feel this respect, they begin to build a relationship with the author.

---

12. Schein, *Humble Inquiry*, 2.
13. Clark, *Writing Tools*, 155.
14. Schein, *Humble Inquiry*, 100.
15. Ibid., 10.

Start a Conversation

Compelling theology cultivates this relationship between the writer and the reader. Great writers make readers feel as if they are sitting next to them telling a story. Great writers make readers feel like the narrative was written just for them. As theologian Thomas Merton believes, great prose makes you, the reader, feel convinced that the author understands you perfectly.[16] Your mission requires you to convince your readers that you understand them perfectly. You need to convince them that you are writing just for them.

This doesn't need to be a literary version of the strained birds-and-bees talk between a parent and a teenager; loosen up and write a chat between two friends. Use conversational language. This doesn't mean dumbing it down; it means talking like "real" people with other "real" people like a friend not a know-it-all boss. Make the reader feel as if they are right next to you. I suggest getting into the flow by writing to yourself.

In the classic *The Elements of Style,* the authors explain "your whole duty as a writer is to please and satisfy yourself, and the true writer always plays to an audience of one."[17] What is important to you? Write about those topics. Anne Lamott suggests, "write about the things that are most important to you. Love and death and sex and survival are important to most of us. Some of us are also interested in God and ecology."[18] Imagine other people similar to yourself. Then, go hang out with them and talk about something meaningful.

Write what you love to read. Each of us knows why we read what we read. We know what we enjoy. We know the difference between the books we read because we have to read them, the books we read because we should read them, and the books we read because we love to read them. Write what you love, and hopefully other people will love it too.

I love the image that Austin Kleon creates when he writes "it's one of my theories that when people give you advice, they're really just talking to themselves in the past."[19] This provides a wonderful image for authors. Imagine sitting on a park bench or in a café with your younger self, a younger self who has not had the leisure of reading and study, who has

16. Merton, *Echoing Silence*, 105.

17. Strunk and White, *The Elements of Style*, 84.

18. Lamott, *Bird by Bird*, 108.

19. Kleon, *Steal Like an Artist*, 1.

not experienced the world as you have, who has not been to the places you have been. What would you talk about? What language would you use? Would you talk about philosophical concepts or practical advice? Much of this depends on you and your personality. How would you talk to yourself, a self without the baggage, wisdom (hopefully), and wit of age? Or would you just listen? This is your intended audience. Talk to them as humans, as fellow pilgrims, as friends.

When we have conversations with friends, we talk about what we know. We share stories about experiences, we catch up on our latest insights, the deals we found at the store, what our families are doing. Write what you know. Your narrative should be based on what you want your reader to experience. Never tell your audience what you can show them. What readers want is a good story that makes them want to read page after page. Collect stories and share them. Don't be afraid to tell a joke or share a gripe. That's what good conversation is all about.

A good conversation should be descriptive not prescriptive. When we write descriptive narrative, we explain concepts to our audience. We use examples and provide insights. We unpack ideas and reveal their strengths and weaknesses. When we write with a prescriptive voice, we try to persuade. A prescriptive narrative focuses on staking a claim, making an argument, and convincing everyone we have the answer. We tend to impose our answers on everyone's questions. When we rely on telling, we sometimes leave out key details that prevent our readers from growing into a more mature faith. A good conversation should inform our audiences rather than tell them what to do or believe. And yes, I see the irony in this, since I am making a prescriptive argument in this book, but I hope readers perceive my openness to different ways of doing and writing theology, especially theology that makes the narrative feel more descriptive.

Also, write from memory. When we have a conversation, we don't tell our friends other peoples' stories, unless they're really juicy. We tell them *our* stories. Be an authentic theologian. Write about what you know—your experiences, your hobbies, your worries, your stress, your family, your loves. Your friends like to hang out with you, not you wearing someone else's personality. If you have survived more than a couple decades in the church, I am sure you have more than enough source material. Conversations that grow out of our memories provide authentic, believable prose that compels readers to keep reading.

Remember, we are not merely one thing. We are a combination of experiences, roles, likes and dislikes. Bring all of this to the conversation. Be a multidimensional author who is not afraid to share truths, including misfortunes and mistakes. Readers don't like perfect authors. Do you enjoy hanging out with a friend who always makes you feel inadequate? Make yourself as real as possible to your readers, just as you make your readers as real as possible to yourself when writing for them. Sit down and have a conversation with your readers.

TAKE A MOMENT TO REFLECT

1. What kind of books do you love to read?

2. If you were sitting on a park bench with your younger self, what would you want to talk about?

Raise Questions; Don't Spoon Feed Answers

Theologians, it isn't our job to fix people. Leave that up to God. The vast majority of readers don't pick up books to be fixed. Writing theology isn't about giving answers. It should be about compelling readers to ask questions. We do try to move our intended readers to action, to change, and to reflect, but this isn't trying to fix them. Theologians Brennan Hill, Paul Knitter, and William Madges argue "faith is seldom certain."[20] This becomes an important reality when writing compelling theology. We need to offer readers a healthy theology that, as Bruce Epperly explains, "gives people a pathway to face tragedy, social change, and injustice with a sense of hope and empowerment."[21] Healthy theology doesn't offer answers; it compels questions, not cynical, hope-killing questions but honest questions offered in love and empowerment.

It is easy to be one of those authors who just tell everyone what to do, what to say, what to believe, but it is more compelling to open deep, thought-provoking questions. Theology should develop our faith; it should facilitate our spiritual journey.[22] Theology that only provides answers is like

20. Hill et al., *Faith, Religion, & Theology*, 11.

21. Epperly, *Process Theology*, 157.

22. Hill et al., *Faith, Religion, & Theology*, 293.

baby food—it doesn't offer a lot to chew on. Asking the right question leads the reader out of their preconceived notions and into the compelling world of possibilities. Make readers think. Believe in their intelligence.

When you cause your readers to think, you create room for readers to grow just as you grow by writing your words. Remember when you were a child and you went shopping for new shoes? The sales person always recommended you buy shoes that had room to grow. Offer ideas that your readers will grow into.

Don't be afraid of doubt. If you aren't sure then share that uncertainty with your readers. Be open, but give readers doubt that they can do something with. Give them doubt that opens questions and creates possibilities, not doubt that crushes and harms as theologians Brennan Hill, Paul Knitter, and William Madges explain,

> Constructive doubt searches sincerely for a deeper understanding, is open to new data, and seriously open to other points of view. Here the statement "I don't know" is sincere and open. . . . Destructive doubt is cynical and even rebellious, rejecting authority and having little respect for the beliefs in question. Here the intent is to get rid of beliefs rather than to gain new understanding of them, to destroy rather than to discover. The statement here is often, "I don't know, and so what?"[23]

Constructive doubt nourishes faith with honest questions. When you allow readers to find their own answers you promote a more mature faith. You can't grow up for them; you can only support them while they are growing up. Growing up is an open-ended process. Shoes that fit one day might be too small the next. Give your intended audience questions to grow into not out of.

Leave room for readers to reflect. This is hard for authors. We learn so much about our subject through reflection and research that we want to share it all. Theologian Terrence Tilley observes "a brilliant theologian may know a great deal about her or his research area. But what s/he can communicate to an audience will depend partly on the capacity they have to hear and absorb what s/he says."[24] We need to understand our intended audience's capacity to grow so we can put the right shoes on their feet. Big enough to fit perfectly by the time they grow of them, but not so big that they look like a penguin waddling around in clown shoes.

23. Ibid., 12.
24. Tilley, *Story Theology*, 58.

Touch Heads and Hearts

Compelling theology doesn't just feed the head, it must also nourish the heart. Theologians Brennan Hill, Paul Knitter, and William Madges note, "human faith involves not only knowledge, but also feelings, decisions, and actions."[25] We need to speak at least as much to our audience's hearts as we write to their heads.[26] Theology without a heart is just mental gymnastics. Show the love. Give readers emotional and rational doorways into the text.

Traditionally, Western society devalues other ways of knowing. We have valued the head but not the heart. Theologian Virginia Phelan suggests this is

> the legacy of Rene Descartes, the seventeenth-century French philosopher who rejected sensory evidence and accepted only the evidence of reason. His "I think; therefore, I am" has guided and constrained Western consciousness, influencing societies (and thus schools) to trust what is linear, analytical, abstract, sequential, rational, and directed, and to distrust what is not-linear, relational, concrete, concurrent, intuitive, and free.[27]

Our theology must value many ways of knowing. We must offer our readers as many avenues to understand as we can. This requires theologians to cross-train themselves. Each and every message we communicate must appeal to both the logical and the creative. It must contain emotional ways of knowing and rational ways of knowing. We must anchor our ideas in both their heads and their hearts.

Consider the Three Publics

In a chapter on the intended audiences for theology, I would be remiss not to mention theologian David Tracy. Tracy argues that "each theologian addresses three distinct and related social realities: the wider society, the academy, and the church."[28] These are three classic audiences for theology: the church, the academy, and society. Tracy calls these publics, but I prefer the simpler term "audiences." You can call it what you like. On a side note, our intended audience is probably just a small group within

25. Hill et al., *Faith, Religion, & Theology*, 9.

26. Jacks, *Just Say the Word!*, 94.

27. Phelan, *Praying in Your Own Voice through Writing*, 7.

28. Tracy, *The Analogical Imagination*, 5.

one of these three meta-groups. But my real point is that we need to be open to all three. And that is hard. Very hard. Most theologians don't even pretend to try to address all three. Many theologians resolve this problem by just choosing one of the three audiences. [29] But Tracy argues that "however personally committed to a single public (society, academy, or church) a particular theologian may be, each strives, in principle and in fact, for a genuine publicness and thereby implicitly addresses all three publics."[30] Tracy is therefore arguing for a unity of audience. All a theologian has to do is write something that successfully speaks to the church, the academy, and society. Easy right?

Let it sink in. Something that successfully communicates with readers from the church, the academy, and society. I suggest you stop reading now and go get a strong drink. If you are home alone, go to a bar; you should never drink alone. If you come from a dry tradition that doesn't believe in alcohol, take a friend, like me, to the bar, have yourself a lemonade without sugar (real lemons), and buy your friend a drink.

South African theologian James Cochrane argues that "all theology . . . must come to terms ultimately with its public character. Having said that, Tracy's terminology of publics, though helpful, is also potentially misleading in several ways."[31] He continues by explaining, "in one sense I confine myself, therefore, to one of Tracy's three reference groups, society. I do so to undermine any separation between society, academy, and church."[32] Cochrane drives Tracy's point home. He argues for the unity of all three and believes theologians must strive to address all three.

Warning: the rest of this chapter only gets harder. Yes, it is definitely time for a drink!

Take a Moment to Reflect

1. What audience is hardest for you to write for?
2. Can writers really write for all three publics? How?

29. Ibid., 51.
30. Ibid., 5–6.
31. Cochrane, *Circles of Dignity*, 122.
32. Ibid., 123.

Surplus of Meaning

The only way to address a unity of audiences requires us to write a surplus of meanings. You have to layer the text. While maintaining accessible language, illustrations, and writing techniques for your intended audience, you must design open possibilities that speak to wider audiences. If this was easy, everyone would be doing it. But many theologians feel content to write for only one of Tracy's publics. Tracy's own texts are densely layered academic tomes that are hardly accessible to wider audiences in the church and society. Tracy writes of the ideal that he doesn't attain. Actually, few theologians attain this ideal. That is the reason for my call for revolution. Tracy's unity of publics is my battle cry. I did warn you that this revolution wasn't going to be easy.

This is like planning a dinner party for all kinds of guests. Meat-lovers, vegetarians, vegans, people with peanut allergies, people who are lactose intolerant, people who won't eat non-sustainable seafood. You've invited them all and all their friends. Now you have to feed them. See, you do need that drink.

To attain a surplus of meaning requires excessive research, experiences, Scripture study, and hours spent composing, revising, and re-revising. I begin with my intended audience and try to compel them into the narrative. Next, I layer in footnotes and references that will attract academic readers, who would probably read it anyway if it had a good plot, but would never admit to reading it to their peers unless it sounded boring. Sprinkle in some practical ideas, creativity, stories, and a plot with a good dose of spiritual reflection to engage a wider audience. Just reach for the ideal. Anyone who finds better approaches, please publish them!

Failure to Communicate

Even with a surplus of meaning, there will be failures to communicate. When I was writing my dissertation, I sent a survey out to a group of clergy. One of the questions I asked them was: "When reflecting upon your working life as a clergy person, what biblical characters do you identity with?" I hoped to get a sense of their metaphorical understanding of their work. I gave them eight possible characters to select and an option to pick someone else and include an explanation. One clergyperson answered, "some days Job, some days Zaccheus (we're coming to your house for lunch!), some days Abraham (entertaining angels), some days Balaam's ass (redirecting a recalcitrant but well-intentioned rider)." I laughed out loud when I read this answer. I loved the story of Balaam's ass as a child, but I had never returned to it as an adult reader.

Balaam's ass! What an answer. The story of Balaam's ass comes from chapter 22 of the book of Numbers. Numbers happens to be one of the least preached and least written about books in the Bible. The Israelites are wandering around the wilderness near the country of Moab. This makes the King of Moab very nervous. He sends a message to Balaam, a prophet, offering to pay him to place a curse on the Israelites. Balaam tells the messengers to stay the night, and he will speak with God.

When God comes to Balaam, Balaam tells God that the King of Moab wants to hire him to place a curse on the Israelites. But God answers: NO. God explains that the Israelites are God's people. They are a blessing. God tells Balaam not to go to the king. Balaam sends the messengers away, but the king sends them back pleading for him to come. Balaam goes to God again, and God tells him, "If the men have come to summon you, get up and go with them; but do only what I tell you to do."

Now comes the part about the ass. Balaam saddles his ass to go to the king. But God wasn't happy about Balaam not listening the first time. So, God sends an angel to block Balaam's way. The angel stands in the road, blocking Balaam's way, with an extended sword. Now the ass sees the angel with the sword and turns off the road, but Balaam doesn't see anything. He just gets mad at the ass and hits her. Again, the angel with the sword blocks the road at a narrow place between two walls. The ass pushes to the side and scrapes Balaam's foot against the wall. Now, Balaam gets really angry. A third time, the angel blocks the road and there is nowhere for the ass to go. The ass stops and lays down. Balaam is so mad that he starts hitting the ass with his staff.

God empowers the ass to speak to Balaam and the ass asks, "What have I done that you have struck me these three times?"

"Because you have made a fool of me! I wish I had a sword in my hand! I would kill you right now!" Balaam screams.

The ass reminds Balaam of the many times she has carried him and of her years of faithful service. Then God allows Balaam to see the angel with the sword, and he understands that his faithful ass has saved him from death three times. After the angel tells Balaam off for beating his ass (you go angel) and not listening to God the first time, the angel instructs Balaam to go to the King of Moab and bless the Israelites.

This is the story of Balaam's ass. The ass suffers because of a failure in communication. She can't explain to Balaam why she isn't doing what he wants or that she is saving his life. Communication breaks down. Theologians are the asses (not to be confused with the helpful ass in this story) when they fail to communicate with their intended audiences. Several major factors cause these failures, and we must work hard to reach our readers in spite of them.

Some days I feel like Balaam's ass. No one understands what I am saying. My readers don't get me. They miss my message. They misinterpret my point. I feel like an ass: sat on, beaten down, and unappreciated. Do you ever feel like Balaam's ass? We carry our readers on journeys that take us months and sometime years to write, and they abandon us every time their phone buzzes with a text message. The breakdown in communication between the writer and the reader has a variety of causes. But I believe the biggest factor is distracted readers.

Take a Moment to Reflect

1. Describe an experience when you felt like Balaam's ass.

2. Do you remember reading a book and felt the author failed you?

Filter the Noise: Keep Them Reading

We live in a world full of distracted readers. Some writers believe distractions are the reader's problem, but I believe they are our problem as writers. Our readers are drowning in information. Their postmodern multitasking minds are attempting to do too many tasks at once and leave them unable to do anything well. The constant flow of interruptions from cell phones, e-mails, social media all keep pulling them away from our words. We have to understand we are competing for our readers' attention. We must compel them back into the story again and again. We compel distracted readers with brevity, with naturally flowing structures, and with clear messages.

Distracted readers require rewards to keep them reading, those gold coins that keep them looking for more. But even distracted readers will stop following a trail of gold coins if the trail seems to go on forever. When they collect too many gold coins to carry, they will stop. According to Joseph McCormack, brevity is the answer. When readers are drowning in information, they will pick the shorter work to read. It is hard enough to compel someone to read at all, but to compel them to read a title that needs a wheelbarrow to haul it around is nearly impossible. Big books don't compel readers unless they come with amazing plots and great characters, so unless you write theology the way J. K. Rowling, Stephen King, or George R. R. Martin write novels, shorter is better.

But brevity is not just about being short. You need to structure your writing projects so they feel brief. McCormack observes, "a media trainer in New York put it to me this way: 'Being brief is not just about time. What's more important is how *long it feels* to the audience.'"[33] The complexity of sentence structures, the length of paragraphs, and the density of the ideas all play into making a work feel long. Know your intended audience. How long do they have to read on any given day? How fast do they read? If you don't know, find out. As writers, this helps us know how long sentences, paragraphs, and chapters should be. Naturally flowing structures guide readers and give them natural opportunities to stop and restart reading. When prose gives readers what they need and feels brief, readers will feel compelled to keep reading.

McCormack also argues that we need to "*make sure no assembly is required. Make it easy to listen and understand by giving all the essential elements logically organized.*"[34] We shouldn't confuse readers. Make the message clear as well as concise. Don't leave readers struggling to understand what you mean. Many of us don't try to confuse our readers, it just happens naturally. We know our content so well that we naïvely believe if we give them all the parts they will see our master plan. We forget to add details, we skip over concepts, we jump around. Confused readers, those who are surrounded by distractions, will become former readers. You will find more recommendations for building beautiful flowing narrative structures and clear messages in chapters 6 and 7.

33. McCormack, *Brief*, 9.
34. Ibid., 215.

The Times They Are a Changin'

Distracted readers are just one of the problems we face as authors. How people read also appears to be changing. This change will impact how we write. Readers read e-books differently than they read print books. The vast majority of theologians produce narratives for linear, paper-based readers, but as readers change how they read, we will need to change too. Joseph McCormack argues that "we are transitioning from a text-based world to a visual one. Screens and interactive media pervade all parts of our lives. Screens are in our homes, our classrooms, our elevators, even our bathrooms. They have replaced phones, books, newspapers, billboards, and printed menus."[35] You must consider how your messages translate from the paper page to the digital page. You must research the reading trends of your intended audience and write to their style and needs. Non-linear models of reading and interactive theology are just two of the possibilities awaiting us.

The social, economic, and environmental realties of our little blue and green planet also point to the changing signs of the time for theological communication. Richard Lischer notes, "after Auschwitz, Hiroshima, Vietnam, Cambodia, Rwanda, all the words sound hollow . . . When the message of Jesus Christ can be Nazified or made the tool of racism, anti-Semitism, apartheid, or capitalism, it is time for preachers to shut up and take stock of themselves."[36] These realities impact your ability to compel readers to read theology. You must take stock of your words and how you converse with your audiences. The future of theological communication will be difficult for theologians, but I find it full of exciting possibilities.

TAKE A MOMENT TO REFLECT:

1. Reflect on how you read: physically, emotionally, intellectually, and spiritually. What do you know about reading?

2. How does understanding how you read help you write for other readers?

3. What realities impact how theology is read today?

35. Ibid., 92.
36. Lischer, *The End of Words*, 5.

Different Generations, Different Readers

Generational gaps are another sign of constant change, but the difficulty in writing for different generations with different beliefs brings another set of challenges. When our points of reference differ from those of our readers, we lose touch with our audiences. Remember your intended audience. What are their points of reference? What anchors their sense of reality, history, and faith? Writer Arthur Plotnik challenges us:

> Writer's—get with it! Are you reaching all those generations out there? The Boomers? The Xers? The Gen-Yers or Echo Boomers or Sreenages, or whatever they're called? And don't forget—Generation Z has arrived, albeit mostly in diapers. The wee Zers may not catch all your nuances; but soon they'll be the generation *du jour*; and you can't afford to be, gasp, Generation Yesterday![37]

There are two major approaches to cause this failure: writing prose that only speaks to one generation and writing prose that attempts to speak to all generations but doesn't anchor itself in the here and now. In my opinion, both options lead to failure. When we only write to one generation or fail to anchor our narratives in the here and now, we fail potential readers. There is a fine line between getting with it and becoming a one-audience theologian. When we become a one-generation author, our audience can never grow. The life span of prose that's jazzed up with the latest fad language and dosed with pop culture references is short. Your prose could be on life-support by the time it's published. As writing expert Arthur Plotnik mentions, we need to reach all those generations out there. And that, my friends, is hard, like jumping-across-the-Grand-Canyon hard.

The opposite problem—failing to anchor our prose in the here and now—may resolve the first problem. When we use generic illustrations instead of contemporary examples and write with a generic vocabulary, we increase the longevity of our prose, but we lose those elements that anchor us to the here and now. This requires a very fine balance. We need to produce prose with theological and linguistic longevity, but still balance our words so they compel readers with relevance to the daily life of today. Maybe it's time for another drink.

Like style, language changes. What readers like now is not what readers will like thirty years from now. When we tour houses, we can point out a 1970s bathroom or a 1950s kitchen. Styles come and go. Luckily, blue shag

---

37. Plotnik, *Spunk & Bit*, 224.

carpet doesn't seem to be coming back anytime soon. But it will someday. Lischer applies this issue to theological narrative when he writes, "this is a beautiful Hebrew sentence that meanders like a brook, but the contemporary hearer is already listening for the punch line or the payoff."[38] This leaves me thinking: well, how do we write compelling theology with all these potential problems? I'm starting to feel like Balaam's ass again.

Define Your Message

In light of the many ways we confuse, lose, and drive our readers away, we can start addressing our failures by knowing our message. Compelling an audience requires intention. Roy Peter Clark notes that "J. K. Rowling began writing the Harry Potter series by crafting the final chapter of the last book and has even revealed the last word: 'scar.'"[39] This requires real intention. This may be rather linear for my cyclical thinking friends, but I believe we need to know where we are going with each writing point. What do you want your audiences to know? If you can't answer this, you are not ready to write.

After you define your message, use timeless methods. Jesus told stories about everyday life with its twists and turns, Homer used adventure stories, and Confucius used mind-bending sayings. Compel readers with what has worked, but with fresh language, illustrations, and your own special voice. You need to give your readers "aha" moments that blend the best of the old with the new.

Remember, you also need passion. Spread excitement, sow enthusiasm. Readers pick up on your emotions. They know when you are excited about your writing. Excitement is contagious, but so are boredom and depression. As E. B. White and William Strunk observe, "who can confidently say what ignites a certain combination of words, causing them to explode in the mind?"[40] The answer is no one, but you need to keep experimenting to find what works for you as a writer and what compels your readers. That is the winning combination. Writing is risk-taking. Compelling your audiences to read requires a little risk on your part as the author.

---

38. Lischer, *The End of Words*, 95.
39. Clark, *Writing Tools*, 188.
40. Strunk and White, *The Elements of Style*, 66.

Conclusion

Readers will interpret our words in ways that we did not intend or expect in our wildest dreams and that's okay. Great theology must always open doors for new and unexpected guests. Give them theology with personality. Re-enchant the world of faith. Re-enchant ecclesiology, pastoral care, or ethics with compelling prose fashioned for an intended audience. The end goal is in the audience. We want them to read and re-read. We want them to come closer to God and closer to each other on this little blue and green planet called earth.

Returning to the story I told at the beginning of this chapter. Did I fail my audience? On that night, I felt I did. But looking back, our conversation opened new doors of questioning for both of us. Our conversation was filled with respect and a welcoming attitude. We were both descriptive and not prescriptive in our messages. We had a conversation, and although it didn't resolve the question, it did open avenues of communication. I wasn't Balaam's ass that night. I was a theologian, working hard to share and grow. I hope he was compelled to keep seeking answers for his questions. I know our conversation compelled me to become a better theologian.

TAKE A MOMENT TO REFLECT

1. What would make you a "better" theologian?

five

Compelling Theology: Writing Techniques

Bring on the heat! Not the Miami Heat, but the tongue-searing, cry-me-a-river heat of a bright red chili pepper. I love hot, spicy food. It's a compulsion. I enjoy the taste of hot jalapenos with their rating of around five thousand SHUs on the Scoville Heat Index. I even enjoy Serrano peppers with their rating of ten to twenty-five thousand SHUs. But the ghost pepper, or the naga jolokia as it is also known, has a heat rating of over one million SHUs; that's a little too spicy for my taste. That kind of heat repels me more than compels me. As I write in chapter 1, the ability to compel is one of three key elements included in writing great theological prose. Compelling writing encompasses an understanding of attributes and techniques that will attract people to become readers of your theological expression. This chapter explores the writing process and techniques that will enable you to write theology that compels readers to read it again and again.

Writing Process: An Introduction

"Almost all good writing begins with terrible first efforts," moans author Anne Lamott.[1] Remember this! And don't despair. Writing is a process. It can feel like a very desperate process, but the process produces pages. The writing process includes five major steps: prewriting, drafting, revising, editing, and publishing. The key is defining the details within the writing process that empower you to write engaging, compelling, and beautiful theology. This isn't easy. Author Marie Arana reminds writers that "there is no one way to approach the writing of a book, unless, of course, you are

1. Lamott, *Bird by Bird*, 25.

producing pulp cookie-cutter versions of the same thing. If you strive to become a real writer, an original, you need to be told clearly: There is no magic formula."[2] While there isn't a magic formula, developing a winning process sure does help. Writing engaging, compelling, and beautiful theology embodies the hard work of craftsmanship.

Prewriting

Prewriting, especially the (pre) pre-writing recommendations that I make in chapters 2 and 3, may seem like a waste of time. After all, they don't produce words on pages. But the proper balance between pre-writing and drafting benefits both processes. Pre-writing gets you ready to write. It embodies the activities you need to create a plan. These activities can include reading, doing research, outlining, brain-storming, or clustering; whatever process works for you, it prepares you for the hard, grueling work of writing.

Pre-writing is the stage when you jump start yourself. It is when you fall in love with your subject or fail to launch. William Zinsser argues that as a writer, you are the one who has to "turn on the switch. Nobody is going to do it for you." He argues that "writers have to jump-start themselves at the moment of performance, no less than actors and dancers and painters and musicians."[3] You have to fire yourself up. Don't just *like* good ideas, you need to fall deeply, passionately *in love* with them. This is what brings on the heat. Readers enjoy reading prose written by writers who love their subjects. Your passion will shine through and compel your readers to consume your words.

Pre-writing starts with two questions, as Pulitzer Prize winning non-fiction author Annie Dillard notes: "Can it be done? And, can I do it?"[4] These questions ring true for any writing project, especially theology. These questions need to be answered in the pre-writing stage. If you answer "yes" to both of them, proceed to your idea. If you answered "no" to either question, go back and find a new idea.

2. Arana, "Introduction," xiv.

3. Zinsser, *On Writing Well*, 243.

4. Dillard, *The Writing Life*, 72.

Finding Ideas

Finding your idea starts the pre-writing process. But novelist Stephen King argues "your job isn't to find these ideas but to recognize them when they show up." He continues, "good story ideas seem to come quite literally from nowhere, sailing at you right out of the empty sky: two previously unrelated ideas come together and make something new under the sun."[5] Great ideas appear before theologians all the time. We just have to train ourselves to recognize them.

Everyday life remains the best source for inspirational, good ideas. Some of the most fruitful moments for me happened while on expressways during traffic jams, in shopping malls, grocery stores, and the waiting rooms at doctors' offices or the court houses, or during activities like cooking, bird-watching, and playing with children at the local playground. Often, I don't even need to leave my backyard before I recognize a great idea. I suggest finding a place where life is happening and ask yourself: What does this mean for me as a person of faith? What does it mean for my community of faith? Try looking deep through your eyes and then try looking deep through other people's eyes. What do they see going on here? Remember the view from the pulpit and the view from the pew all look out over the sanctuary, but they are radically different perspectives. You can also refer back to chapter 3 and re-read the sections on sources for theology. The possibilities for finding ideas are endless.

Controlling Ideas

Once you find an idea, you need to keep it from running away. One piece of writing, even an epic poem, can never cover every detail. Writers need to control their ideas. Mary Gordon offers the metaphor of building a fence. She writes: "a novelist builds a fence enclosing a certain area of the world and then calls it his or her subject."[6] A large aspect of pre-writing is narrowing your topic. Think small, bite-size. Every writing project must be reduced before it is manageable. Look for the stark simplicity of one idea and begin exploring.

After you narrow the idea down, try cutting to the root of the issue. Writer Annie Dillard explains this idea by using the image of splitting wood

5. King, *On Writing*, 37.
6. Gordon, "Getting Here from There," 26.

to explain getting to the root of an idea. She writes: "aim for the chopping block. If you aim for the wood, you will have nothing. Aim past the wood, aim through the wood; aim for the chopping block."[7] Cut down to the idea underneath. Ask yourself what is going on under the surface? What am I trying to show my audience? What is the key to understanding this idea theologically? I suggest writing into the idea. Begin exploring everything you know or think you know about this idea. Use your writing to think. Writing is thinking, but writing works better than thinking in our heads because we can't forget our insights when we have a written record. Dig through the levels to refine this idea: backhoe, shovel, hand trowel, and brush until you reach that pocket of pure potential. Write about your topic by exploring your thoughts, worries, questions, hunches; raise doubts; talk to people, both insiders and outsiders; and flesh out your idea.

TAKE A MOMENT TO REFLECT

1. What writing projects do you remember getting out of control?
2. How did you lose control?

Plan but Be Free

Next, create a plan. Plans should always be a work in process. As William Zinsser reminds us, "don't become the prisoner of a preconceived plan."[8] Don't set your plans in stone. Write your plan so that it may be changed easily and quickly. God is great at changing plans. And as a great planner, it has always frustrated me that God always seems to tell me that my plans need to change at the last minute. Come on God, a little notice would be nice. Notice would give me time to develop a resistance plan for God's plan, which is probably why I never get early notice. Writers need to allow their plans to develop naturally.

Novelist E. L. Doctorow once said that "writing a novel is like driving a car at night. You can see only as far as your headlights, but you can make the whole trip that way."[9] This is natural development. This means

7. Dillard, *The Writing Life*, 59.
8. Zinsser, *On Writing Well*, 53.
9. Lamott, *Bird by Bird*, 18.

that planning doesn't end after the pre-writing stage; planning is only the beginning. In planning, I like to visually map out how I am going to bring my idea into conversation with the sources of theology. Then, I just keep writing into the subject as I add conversation partners. Finally, I create an outline of the themes I discover, one that is always evolving as I move the project forward. Don't allow an outline, or any plan, to become a prison cell. Follow the curves of the road as your car's headlights reveal them. Don't be afraid to explore a side street. If it proves to be a dead end, just circle back to the main idea. If it proves to be a shortcut, follow it.

Drafting

The next step in the writing process is drafting. How do you write? One word at a time.[10] Drafting puts words into sentences, sentences into paragraphs, and paragraphs into coherent order. Drafting is what most people consider real writing. But the writing process of drafting contains several major considerations.

The first major consideration is your schedule. What is your writing schedule? I am a big believer in writing every day. Anne Lamott explains, "I wrote every night for an hour or more, often in coffeehouses with a notepad and my pen, drinking great quantities of wine because this is what writers do; this was what my father and all his friends did."[11] There is no right way to draft, and there is no wrong way to draft if you are producing usable pages. I consider five thousand words to be a very productive day. But even if you produce one good page a day that still generates a lot of pages over one year. Creating a writing plan means budgeting your time, creating a schedule, and forcing yourself to put your fingers on the keyboard.

There are two types of writers: Gushers and Bleeders.[12] Gushers pour words onto the page at an amazing rate. Words, sentences, and paragraphs just seem to flow out of Gushers. Because Gushers write quickly they generate a lot of pages. But they also spend more time in the revising and editing stages because their pages are raw and need more development. They need to re-work the material more. Bleeders produce pages slowly, sometime painfully slowly. Bleeders' pages are often more carefully designed and crafted, but they often produce less than one page a day. It doesn't matter

10. King, *On Writing*, 156.
11. Lamott, *Bird by Bird*, xxii.
12. Fickett, "Gushers and Bleeders," 5.

what type you are. In the end, both types will likely invest the same amount of time to craft engaging, compelling, and beautiful theological prose. They just invest their time in different parts of the writing process. Don't feel bad if you are a Bleeder who is sitting next to a Gusher who can write ten pages in an hour while you can only write three. After revising and editing, the Gusher will probably have three pages too.

Your writing location and time are the heartbeat of the second consideration. Novelist Stephen King argues that you need a room with a door and the determination to shut that door.[13] Writers need to be able to concentrate. Paradoxically, to write about life, we often need to withdraw into a room of our own. Every writer is different in their need for time and space when drafting; but you need to figure out what your brain requires to concentrate. Interruptions cause many writers to lose their train of thought. Control interruptions. Thomas Merton reminds us that "silence is the mother of speech."[14] Find your silence.

I write in an office with my blinds down but still allowing sunlight into the room, background music, and a pot of tea. Other writers can suspend the world around them and write in coffee shops filled with people and conversations. Discover what works for you. Learn to control the interruptions that you can control and accept the interruptions that are uncontrollable. Preventing writing burnout becomes critical after spending day after day in this room. I suggest working in a colorful, light-filled, and relaxing environment, working on one task at a time, taking stretching breaks every hour, and exercising after your writing time each day. I love walking after writing. Find what works for you and put it into action.

The writer's job during this time is to fashion a draft. Annie Dillard explains "when you write, you lay out a line of words. The line of words is a miner's pick, a woodcarver's gouge, a surgeon's probe. You wield it, and it digs a path you follow. Soon you find yourself deep in a new territory."[15] This is drafting: putting one word on a page and then adding the word that comes next. Follow the path your words create.

Your first draft is your zero draft. For me, a zero draft means taking the outline I produced during pre-writing and dropping in all the quotes and insights I gained during my research where I engaged with the sources of theology. I just add everything I might need into the outline. A zero draft

13. King, *On Writing*, 157.
14. Merton, *Echoing Silence*, 19.
15. Dillard, *The Writing Life*, 3.

will only make sense to the writer who wrote it. To the outsider, a zero draft looks like a jumble of ideas, quotes, and random thoughts. But to the writer, a zero draft is a mix of all the raw ingredients that will be blended together to make the cake.

Next comes the first draft. Anne Lamott reminds us that we need "shitty first drafts. All good writers write them. This is how they end up with good second drafts and terrific third drafts."[16] In this draft, you pour out your heart, soul, and mind. You begin connecting ideas. You roam all over the place, building bridges between concepts. Expressing old concepts in fresh language. You read a lot and you write a lot. And then the fun begins. Your job in the second draft is to determine where you are going. Define your message. Your job in the third and subsequent drafts is to get your reader to that destination. But you need to decide, are you going by the fastest route, the shortest route, or the scenic route? In the next chapter, as we explore the concept of beautiful theological prose, we will shape this language.

During drafting, two sections demand extra time and effort. Your opening and closing sections are critical for the success of your project. Your opening must grab your reader and compel them into the prose. It needs to hook readers' attention and funnel their focus into the body of your work. Strong openings may start a fight, jump right to the middle, build suspense, or create a story, but they must capture your readers' attention quickly and efficiently. I often suggest writing a rough introduction when you start drafting, and when the rest of the project is done, go back and give the project a front door that pulls readers into the rest of the story.

The conclusion is the second most critical section. Conclusions need to be inviting and informative. Never just stop writing when you finish your last point. Your readers deserve better than that. Conclusions need to open up the realm of possibilities rather than restrict meaning. They need to inspire and motivate readers to reflect and to act.

TAKE A MOMENT TO REFLECT

1. Do you love or hate drafting? Why?

---

16. Lamott, *Bird by Bird*, 21.

Revising and Editing

I am not going to write much about revision here because Gricel spends a whole chapter on revising and editing later in this book. Although revising and editing are often lumped together, they are different processes. Revising and editing represent steps in the writing process that you should not expect to be able to do on your own. All writers need help here. But you as the author must be the final judge. Accept feedback graciously but don't follow advice blindly.

Revision captures the step in the writing process when you change content, rearrange the flow of ideas, delete unnecessary even if brilliantly written paragraphs, and add depth and dimension to your ideas. Revision is also where you rewrite sentences, paragraphs, and entire sections to improve their clarity and structure to give your reader a smooth reading experience that compels them to keep reading. You revise not to shape the narrative but to discover what the shape is. It is like crafting a sculpture; you chip away at the excess and find the form within the rock. Stephen King provides an equation for successful revising and editing: "2nd Draft = 1st Draft – 10%."[17] He believes that as you revise and edit, your text should be more distilled. You find shortcuts to present the same message in fewer words. After fully revising and editing, a twenty-page draft should drop to around eighteen pages (which is ten percent less for non-mathematical types like me).

Editing encompasses the processes of proofreading for grammar, usage, and mechanics mistakes. You edit to polish the prose and make the reading experience as clear as possible for your readers. Readers who feel confused become former readers. When you edit keep asking: How can I make this clearer for my readers? And please remember that correct grammar, usage, and mechanics have nothing to do with your ability to minister or the quality of your faith lives. No writer gets everything perfect the first time, and most of us never get it perfect even when we get it published.

Theologians need to frame their revising and editing work in a spiritual light. Diane Glancy explains that "I think in terms of revision because I have been revised. As a Christian, I feel that I have started over and over, continuing one development after another. . . . I see new ways of doing things I had not thought of before, or new ways of thinking I had not realized. I desire to be rewritten, so to speak. *Don't leave me as I am* has been

---

17. King, *On Writing*, 282.

a way of opening prayer."[18] Revising and editing are the essence of compelling theology. They remind us that writing really means rewriting. They embody craftsmanship. Working and reworking with the final goal of a happy reader.

Publishing

God does not give us the ability and call to write and expect us to waste the gift. Publishing is the final step in the writing process. Don't invest hours, blood, sweat, and tears on a piece of writing only to stick it in a desk drawer or save it in a computer file never to be seen or read. After you have written theology, you need to share it. You need to publish it. You must share it. It is imperative!

Publishing has changed radically in the last ten years with new forms of electronic media. Publishing is not just about finding a publisher who will put your theology into print; rather, publishing is about reaching your intended audience. There are two major considerations at this point: cost point and accessibility. Can your intended audience afford your words if you publish them with this publisher? And will your intended audience find your words with this publisher?

Next, consider the publisher's mission. Does your work fit into their scope? Don't offer your work to a publisher if your work doesn't fit their guidelines. If they don't publish dissertations, don't offer them your dissertation. If they don't publish novels, don't send your novel. If they ask for one sample chapter, don't e-mail twenty. Search for the best fit. Don't shoot for the biggest or most famous publisher right away. But don't just self-publish because you fear a publisher will make you work harder. Write a rationale for why your writing project fits for this publisher.

Then, be ready and willing to work with an editor. Working with a good editor is a blessing. A good editor defines a professional. They bring fresh eyes to your project. They can help you refine your work and bring clarity to your potential readers. It is always a process of give and take and of being open to changes that can improve your text. I read several novelists and theologians who have become so famous that they are allowed to ignore their editors. Their novels and texts become longer and larger. They wander all over the place because they don't have the corrective influence

18. Glancy, "After the Fire of Writing," 199.

of a good editor who has the power to make them listen. Don't be afraid of receiving an editor's insights and making changes.

Publishing also requires you to put yourself out there and to face the "r" word: rejection. Every writer receives rejection notices. A rejection notice isn't a message from God saying you're not good enough. Publishers have many reasons for not accepting a work; don't take it personally. Don't burn your manuscript in a ritualistic way and curse the publisher! Don't burn your manuscript at all. Try another publisher. Try rewriting your manuscript to improve it before you try again. Just keep trying. If you receive a note from an editor who seems to have actually read your work, without trying to get them to reconsider, ask them for advice on improving your writing style. Also, thank everyone who reads your writing. They gave your words their gift of time.

Take a Moment to Reflect

1. What is your best experience with rejection?

Writing Process Conclusions: Learn by Doing

The only way to write theology is to write it and then discover what you have done. We learn to write by writing. We get better with practice. Hopefully, every time we rewrite a draft we improve it. Writer Natalia Goldberg suggests that "learning to write is not a linear process. There is no logical A-to-B-to-C way to become a good writer."[19] But keep writing, keep reading about writing, and keep trying to become a better writer. We learn by doing. Work the process: prewriting, drafting, revising, editing, and publishing.

Writing Techniques

After you learn the five steps of the writing process, you need to begin addressing writing techniques. Compelling theology requires great writing techniques as well as inspiration. We as writers of theology must fight our way out of complacency. Complacency happens because writers, like most humans, feel weighted down by burdens that consume their time. And

19. Goldberg, *Writing Down the Bones*, 4.

don't forget the reality of our own laziness. Once you begin writing, it is easy to write with the same technique over and over, to overuse the same paragraph pattern, and employ the same type of illustrations (or no illustrations) over and over. Never let the status quo win when writing about something as amazing and powerful as God. Even theology needs plots. Theologians make God boring all the time with bad prose. Compelling theology needs complex characters, exciting twists, interesting developments, and fascinating insights. Theologians need to experiment with many writing techniques and approaches to fashion compelling theology; the key remains to capture and hold your reader's attention. And writing techniques provide a tool box full of methods to accomplish this.

Take a Moment to Reflect

1. When you read, what writing technique do you hate?
2. Have you used a writing technique that failed? What caused it to fail?

Genre

Understanding your genre gives you a great doorway into planning your writing techniques. Answer: rap, Impressionism, science fiction, and romantic comedy. Question: What are genres? Genre means a classification system to group materials that share characteristics. We have genres in music, art, fiction, and movies to name a few, but theologians also have different theological genres, such as sermons, spiritual journey novels, and prayers. Genres can be a blessing and a curse to theologians.

Each genre comes with certain reader expectations as well as particular structures and techniques. These structures and techniques force the writer to examine their writing and to rewrite, which is a blessing. The free-writing, stream-of-consciousness style that characterizes much of the writing in the last ten years gives writers incredible freedom. With this freedom, creative writers who have the time can produce stunning, innovative forms of theology. Unfortunately, writers under the pressures of time and the requirement to publish have spewed out technically correct but dry, lifeless prose. The power of a genre forces writers to go back and pay attention. A sermon shouldn't sound like a research paper and vice versa. The more structured the characteristics of a genre the more careful a writer has to be. Try writing a sonnet, fourteen lines of agony and ecstasy as you painstakingly pour over each word to make your meanings fit into the structure. But when you do it right, you know you have crafted something special. Don't be afraid to blend genres together to mix and match and make something new.

Take a Moment to Reflect

1. What is your favorite genre?
2. What makes it so attractive to you?

Disruptive Ideas

Another technique, disruptive ideas capture the attention of many readers. Theologian Melinda McGarrah Sharp explains, "disruptive moments provoke us to contemplate the loss of a person, a state of being, a way of life, a particular vision of the future. In moments of crisis, experiencing a disruption on the level of human existence leads to places of deep vulnerability."[20] A disruptive idea explodes as a phrase or image that brings a reader to a dead stop. The reader can't believe what she or he just read. It startles, shocks, and blows readers away with its profound implications. In the beginning, disruptive ideas might confuse them. A disruptive idea messes with readers' minds and forces them to slow down and rethink the idea. Disruptive ideas often connect ideas that look very different, or create metaphors when the "is not" element seems greater than the "is like" aspect. Read this wonderful passage by Hillel Levine. He writes,

> My response is not that God has retired to Miami Beach, or that God neglects the world, or that God has become impotent in old age. My response is that God, as a very precious gift, gives people freedom, gives people commandments, gives people a sense of right and wrong, gives people a passion for life, all of which can be distorted or perverted, but nevertheless people are given freedom. People are free to create Auschwitzes. People are free to create the Beethoven symphonies. . . . We have to understand those moments and those contradictions. That's the raw material.[21]

20. Sharp, *Misunderstanding Stories*, xi.
21. Levine, "In Search of Sugihara," 71.

As I argued earlier, good theology is less about offering good answers; rather, good theology provokes deep, profound questions. Disruptive ideas demand readers to ask deep, passionate questions. They force readers to explore rather than just passively accept the concept. What were the disruptive ideas in Levine's passage? No matter how many times I read it, I always stop and reflect when I reach the image of God as a retiree on Miami Beach, of God becoming impotent in God's old age, and the image of people being free to create their own Auschwitzes. They are disruptive ideas that capture my attention. They make me stop and ask, "Could this be right?" Disruptive ideas force readers to stop and question. Question their reality, question their assumptions, question their beliefs, question if they are asking the right question. As James Calvin Schaap explains, "the best creative nonfiction, like the best fiction, begins in questions, not answers. Always leave space for the reader's participation. How much? That's for you and your audience to determine."[22] When you think about your potential audience, what is going to make them stop and think? Fashion disruptive ideas to compel readers to reconsider, to pause, to think wow this writer might have something important here.

Storytelling

Once upon a time, when his community faced a crisis, Rabbi Abraham went to the sacred location in the woods, kindled the sacred fire, and recited the words of the sacred payer as his ancestors in the faith had taught him. And God heard, and the community was saved. Many, many years later, Rabbi Abraham's great-grandson Rabbi Issac faced another crisis in the community. He couldn't go to the sacred location in the forest because it had been forgotten, so he built the sacred fire, and recited the words of the sacred payer as his ancestors in the faith had taught him. And God heard, and the community was saved. Decades later, as his community faced a crisis, Rabbi Jacob couldn't go to the sacred location in the forest because it had been forgotten, and he couldn't kindle the sacred fire because those skills had been lost, but he did recite the words of the sacred payer as his ancestors in the faith had taught him. And God heard, and the community was saved. Centuries later and thousands of miles away, Rabbi Hannah, a descendent of Rabbis Abraham, Isaac, and Jacob, faced a crisis in her community. She couldn't go to the sacred location in the forest because it had

22. Schaap, "Deeper Subjects," 92.

been forgotten, and she couldn't kindle the sacred fire because those skills had been lost. She didn't know the words of the sacred prayer because they had been lost. So she told the stories of Rabbi Abraham, Rabbi Issac, and Rabbi Jacob, and God heard, and the community was saved.[23]

Stories are that powerful. As a writer of theology, you can never go wrong by telling or, as I have done here, retelling a story. Often, when other forms of theology are not gentle enough or will cause immediate opposition, stories can break down barriers. I suggest reading the story of prophet Nathan when he faced King David over the king's adultery and murder. He told a story that stopped the king from immediately killing the messenger and forced the king to face the reality of his situation. People remember stories: the scenes, characters, plot, and action. Stories create empathy and fellowship. As Virginia Phelan reminds us, "stories help people see their choices."[24]

Stories are not just illustrations of the "true" theological message in a piece of writing; they are theology. Stories open realms of possibility.

As a technique, storytelling empowers theologians to produce beautiful narratives that stick in people's memories. As a storyteller, don't be afraid to mine traditions from around the world and retell old stories in a new light with your voice and your style. But as you grow in this technique, don't be afraid to write your own stories with plots and characters and action. Storytelling skills takes practice to develop but the time is a great investment in the faith.

Take a Moment to Reflect

1. When you were a child, what was your favorite story?
2. If you don't include stories in your writing project, why?

Metaphors

In both storytelling and in creating disruptive ideas, metaphors shoot up as an important technique for writers of theology. As Anne Lamott explains, "metaphors are a great language tool, because they explain the unknown

---

23. My own retelling of a parable from Metz, *Faith in History and Society*, 274. Metz retells it from a version by Martin Buber.

24. Phelan, *Praying in Your Own Voice Through Writing*, 34.

in terms of the known. But they only work if they resonate in the heart of the writer. So I felt a little understaffed here, loving the metaphor when I came upon it, wanting to work with it, and yet not loving to garden."[25] All religious language is metaphorical. We can't see God, we can't taste faith, we can't touch salvation, we can't smell the Holy Spirit. But theologians can engage beautiful and ugly metaphors and similes to translate the language of faith onto the page.

Metaphors make readers stop and consider how the "is like" and "is not like" of each metaphor relates to the subject. Metaphors transfer aspects of the metaphorical object onto the subject. For example, Jesus the Good Shepherd is a metaphor. I have never liked this metaphor; mainly because I know how smelly and stupid sheep are, so I don't like being compared to one. But it is a widely used metaphor. Jesus is not really a good shepherd; rather, to the writers he behaves *like* a good shepherd.

Sidebar: When you use the "like" you are making your expression into a simile, which is a type of metaphor.

Theologians use the metaphor of Good Shepherd because it helps readers understand what the writer is trying to convey about Jesus. This metaphor empowers the audience to transfer their understanding of a good shepherd onto the subject of discussion, which is Jesus. As writers of theology, try not to keep reusing the same old metaphors again and again because they become old and stale. When readers see the same metaphor over and over, they stop thinking about it. Grow new metaphors that relate to your cultures, your realities, and your experiences. Fresh, unexpected language compels readers to slow down and think. New metaphors cause people to stop and consider the possibilities and implications of your insights.

TAKE A MOMENT TO REFLECT

1. Consider these metaphors: DJ Jesus dubbing some tunes, trashman Jesus picking up the garbage, Jesus the tree hugger telling an oak he loves her.

2. What is your reaction? Why?

Go, therefore, and create new metaphors. New metaphors are a great writing technique to capture readers' attention and make them think.

25. Lamott, *Bird by Bird*, 77.

Concrete Details

Concrete details, like concrete, make ideas stronger. As a writing technique, concrete details sink deep in the minds of readers. Writing about abstract concepts feels easier than describing actual relationships, experiences, and real objects. Helen Sword calls concrete details "the stylish writer's magic bullet."[26] One of the easiest to use but hardest techniques to master is writing with concrete details. Anne Lamott writes the following passage:

> Life is lukewarm enough! Give us a little heat! If I'm going to read about a bunch of people who drive Volkswagen and seem to have mostly Volkswagen-sized problems, and the writer shows them driving around on top of the ice, I want a sense that there's a lot of very, very cold water down below.[27]

Examine the concrete details here. The people are not just driving a car. They drive a Volkswagen. And they aren't just driving the Volkswagen on a road. No, they are driving it on an icy bridge. There isn't just water below; it is a lot of bone-chilling water. (And yes, I am adding details to Anne Lamott's example.) These are concrete details. Concrete details make writing heat up. Natalia Goldberg explains why concrete details feel so important. She writes, "sense memories are a way to anchor us in the present and to open the past."[28] These concrete details anchor the minds of your readers in your narrative. Concrete details cause readers to make emotional, intellectual, and spiritual connections. They stir up memories. They compel readers to keep reading and then to read it again.

Concrete details show rather than just tell. Don't tell readers about justice; show them justice. Why tell your readers about an abstract concept like justice or friendship when you can show them the concept in action. Jesus didn't just tell his audience that it was important to feed the hungry; he took fish and five loaves of bread and fed them. Here is an example of telling versus showing from my spiritual hometown Detroit, Michigan:

- (Telling): The 1950s were a decade of economic problems in the city of Detroit.

- (Showing): During the 1950s, the city of Detroit suffered four major economic recessions. The city lost over 100,000 manufacturing jobs.

---

26. Sword, *Stylish Academic Writing*, 173.
27. Lamott, *Bird by Bird*, 197.
28. Goldberg, *Thunder and Lightning*, 30.

The Murray Auto Body Plant, the Packard Plant, and the Studebaker Plant all closed, and employment at the Rouge River industrial complex fell from over eighty thousand people to only thirty thousand workers by 1960. By 1957, there were 9.9 million square feet of empty factory space in Detroit.

Both of these statements give readers the same core facts on Detroit's economic problems during the 1950s. But the showing statement provides concrete details that drive the reality of the situation deep into the reader's mind. However, be careful not to give your readers unnecessary details. If I added that the southern segment of the I-75 expressway, which is called the Walter P. Chrysler Freeway in Detroit, was built in the 1950s, it would give readers unnecessary details that fail to add anything to the theme of economic problems. Unnecessary details do nothing to advance the core message. If your focus is on people acting as the hands of Jesus in the world, then focus your concrete details on their hands and not their eyebrows. Feed your audience a good, balanced diet of concrete details that compel readers to keep reading and to think.

Other Writing Techniques

Writers can and do employ a variety of other writing techniques to compel their readers to keep reading. Below are some techniques that you might wish to try:

- *In Media Res:* starting the story in the middle and then using a flashback or other technique to fill in the details.

- Alliteration: using the same sound at the beginning of several consecutive words such as: repent, receive, and rejoice.

- Apaphora: using a series of repeating words at the beginning of a phrase for example: love is patient, love is kind, love is not envious nor boastful.

- Homoioteleuton: creating the opposite of apaphora by using a series of repeating words at the end of a phrase for example: when I was a child, I spoke like a child, I thought like a child, I reasoned like a child.

- Personification: giving human-like characteristics to non-human or even non-living items such as: the stones will shout out.

- Oxymoron: bringing together two words or concepts that seem to be opposite, such as: deafening silence.

- Leitworstil: using a repeating word or image to express the theme of the piece.

- Framing: engaging a single scene, image, or concept that appears at both the beginning and the end of the writing project to frame it.

- Catacosmesis: listing statements "in descending order of importance, often ending with a surprising triviality: I ask for peace, prosperity, and a bagel with cream cheese."[29]

- Enallage: using "one part of speech for another, such as a noun or adjective for a verb: Grammar? I'll grammar you!"[30]

- Closed circle or "bookend:" happens when "the ending echoes or completes the opening: Yes, 'once upon a time there was a poor widow with an only son named Jack.' Now it's poor Jack who faces time—for theft and tax fraud—in a kingdom where beans don't count."[31]

- Legacy: occurs when the closings offers advice to the reader.[32]

- Defamiliarization: taking something familiar to your readers and making it into something unexpected.

- Familiarization: taking something familiar to your readers and showing them they really don't know how strange and complex it really is.

Other writing techniques you may try include humor (including parody, hyperbole, and irony), epiphany, mooreeffoc, flashback, flash-forward, and foreshadowing. But always remember that effective writing techniques provide clarity and expand meaning rather than baffling your readers and restricting meaning. Above all else, don't confuse your readers. Confused readers give up. Yes, I know that I said this before. But it's important. And I want everyone to remember. Confused readers give up. Good writing techniques compel readers to read on not stop. Take a stab at a new technique today. Go write something.

29. Plotnik, *Spunk & Bit*, 13.
30. Ibid.
31. Ibid., 143.
32. Ibid.

It's a Craft, Not an Art

Writing compelling theology is a craft not an art. And as with any craft, the more you practice the better you will become. Good writing does not come naturally. It requires hard work, long hours, tears, and sweat. William Zinsser reminds us that "writing is hard work. A clear sentence is no accident. Very few sentences come out right the first time, or even the third time. Remember this in moments of despair. If you find that writing is hard, it's because it *is* hard."[33] But we keep writing and rewriting, until it all comes together organically with body, mind, and soul. I feel that because I am not a good writer, I invest more time and effort into my writing than I would if it flowed. The distance between being an average writer and becoming a good writer is measured in dedication to the craft.

Other Writing Considerations

I have three other compelling writing considerations to explore. These are not true writing techniques. They are approaches to writing theology that compel readers. Silence embodies the first of these considerations. Gustavo Gutierrez notes that "theology is discourse that is continually enriched by silence."[34] In writing, silence is the space between your ideas that allows readers to process what you are presenting. Silence on the page leaves room for readers' brains, souls, and hearts to encounter the subjects. If the density becomes too thick and you overwhelm the readers, they will miss key concepts and maybe lose the depths of your insights. But if the density is too thin, they might lose interest and stop reading. As Lynn Nelson explains, "our words must have silence around them or they, too, lose their meaning."[35] Readers must be able to hear themselves. Silence on paper encapsulates discovering the right balance between presenting a concept, illustrating that concept with writing techniques, and knowing when to move on to the next concept. Putting silence on the page is a skill that may take years to hone.

I know of four methods to put silence on the page. First, theologians need to know their intended audiences. Density refers to your ratio of new

33. Zinsser, *On Writing Well*, 9.
34. Gutiérrez, *We Drink From Our Own Wells*, 136.
35. Nelson, *Writing and Being*, 50.

ideas to amount of words. Introducing fifty new subjects within five hundred words drowns a reader. But only exploring one idea for five hundred words might leave your readers feeling like they are swimming in the kiddy pool. What kind of density are they expecting? Know how much silence you need to leave before jumping to the next, new concept. Second, the use of headings and subheadings create natural stopping points for readers to pause and reflect. Third, structured transitions signal the reader that you are moving to a new idea. This gives readers a sign to stop and consider your point. (Warning, structured transition coming.) Finally, theologians must learn how to space their ideas with quotes from other sources. Back-to-back quotes are always a bad idea; back-to-back long quotes will overwhelm your voice. You will lose yourself and be lost behind someone else's mask. Don't lose your voice. Don't allow your voice to be taken from you. Employ all of these techniques to build silence around your ideas. Silence compels readers to notice your important points.

I also want us to consider how we use our sources. In many academic fields, scholars are trained to critically read other sources to find their holes and limitations. Then they argue how their brilliant work fills these holes and overcomes these limitations. In other words, they are building their arguments on their perceived failures of others. Theologians need to write out a positive point-of-view instead of this negative deconstruction. There are holes and limitations in theologies all over the place. Instead of attacking these holes as opportunities to show how much we know and how much better we can do it, theologians should work from a positive framework of filling-in and building-up. The holes we find give us an opportunity to make all of theology stronger. Don't write from a negative perspective; build from a positive perspective. It's more compelling.

I want to offer one final consideration for writers of theology. Don't use theory to cover your theological ass. Don't use other people's theories as an excuse to not do the hard lifting that theology requires. Just don't drop a reference to a theory and hope no one figures out that you didn't do your homework. If you don't want to put the time and effort into writing compelling theology, then don't write theology.

Writer's Block

Finally, you can't compel readers if you aren't writing. Writer's block is our kryptonite. It stops us mid-sentence. It drains a writer's will and vision. It turns fertile fields of thought into wastelands. And it must be addressed before it takes power over you before it causes your brain to cramp and your fingers to freeze. The primary cause of writer's block is perfection. Anne Lamott observes that "perfectionism is the voice of the oppressor, the enemy of the people."[36] We must fight! Just keep reminding yourself: there is no such thing as perfection. Compel yourself to write. Overcome your crippling quest for perfection.

The second major cause of writer's block is fear. The first type of fear comes from anticipatory grief. We anticipate the pain deep in our gut about how we will feel writing about this experience. And it makes us avoid writing. Anne Lamott argues that pain, losses, and disappointments cause our writing muscles to cramp. She writes,

> They cramp around our wounds—the pain from our childhood, the losses and disappointments of adulthoods, the humiliations suffered in both—to keep us from getting hurt in the same place again, to keep foreign substances out. So those wounds never have a chance to heal. . . . In some cases we don't even know that the wounds and the cramping are there, but both limit us. They keep us moving and writing in tight worried ways. They keep us standing back or backing away from life, keep us from experiencing life in a naked and immediate way.[37]

The second source grows from our fears of not being good enough. We don't believe in our hearts that anything we could write will ever be worth publishing so we don't start. Why would your mind put in the heavy lifting of writing if your heart doesn't believe your words will ever see readers? Don't stop just because you are crying and bleeding, keep writing. The more you practice the better you will become at confronting these fears.

I offer three remedies for writer's block. First, continue to work and rework your raw material over and over again in hope that it will break loose. We learn by doing. Try playing with syntax, break open grammar, or delete all the punctuation marks and rebuild your piece. Secondly, I suggest working on the mundane writing tasks. They need to be done anyway, so spend a day correcting your footnotes, building your bibliography, checking your quotes, and rewriting sentences to get rid of weak verbs. Thirdly, I recommend taking a day long vacation from your current project and

36. Lamott, *Bird by Bird*, 28.
37. Ibid., 30.

writing something completely different. If you are writing prose, write poetry. If you are writing a sermon, try a short story.

But the best method to address writer's block is to vaccinate yourself against this plague. The novelist Ernest Hemingway offers the best vaccination. He suggests that "the best way is always to stop when you are going good and when you know what will happen next."[38] This way you can drop right back into the flow the next day. I recommend never stopping at the end of a section or a chapter; rather, stop mid section and leave yourself some notes about where it is going. Then the next day, you continue on without stopping. Stop writer's block before it starts. Compel yourself.

TAKE A MOMENT TO REFLECT

1. What is stopping you from writing?

Conclusion

Each time we sit down in front of a blank screen or fresh page, a new journey is in front of us. You can go anywhere. The possibilities are endless and the potential infinite. To compose compelling prose, we need to work the writing process without skipping steps. You must explore writing techniques that will make your readers excited to read more. Good theology brings the heat, but only enough to compel, not enough to repel. In the next two chapters, Gricel and I will explore various processes to shape beautiful theological prose from your already engaged and compelling draft.

38. Hemingway, *Ernest Hemingway on Writing*, 41.

An Epistle to Dissertation Candidates

Dear Brothers and Sisters,

You are not alone. God has called you to stand and write during a critical period for the church. Secularization has pushed theology out from her position as queen of the academy.

The church as a whole is broke. Overall, our finances will not support the structures we have built. Our infrastructure is crumbling. Abuse and scandal have diminished our public influence. We have lost power. We have lost privilege. We have lost influence. Not since before Emperor Constantine has the Western Christian tradition's existence been so marginalized by Western mainline society. This is great! It excites me to be writing theology at this time. And I hope it excites you too.

We are no longer prisoners to the empire's power, privilege, and influence. We need new vocabulary and new metaphors to process our roles in postmodern society, if indeed we are postmodern. Our writers will need to discern this new language. Push it, examine it, and probe it. Let your writing show your bewilderment and persistence. Don't get lost in building mazes of abstract language. Write for the head and the heart with clarity and passion. Lead. Empower. Write. As theologian Kathleen Norris argues,

> Language used truly, not mere talk, neither propaganda, nor chatter, has real power. Its words are allowed to be themselves, to bless or curse, wound or heal. They have the power of a "word made flesh," of ordinary speech that suddenly takes hold, causing listeners to pay close attention, and even to release bodily sighs— whether of recognition, delight, grief, or distress.[1]

This real power doesn't embody the language of empire. It doesn't set us up as *the* voice; rather, it enables us to be *a* voice. Often, doctoral prose is a

---

1. Norris, *Amazing Grace*, 9.

"voiceless prose"[2] that attempts to hide the author. Don't hide. Remember your voice is not neutral; you are part of your prose. Don't be satisfied with producing mediocre, weak, wishy-washy prose. Stand up and let your readers see you.

During this phase of your writing career, learn to work with others. Learn to work in groups. We do not like or trust groups, and I have often felt that the hardest aspect of being a theologian is being forced to work with fellow Christians. Theologians don't need to prove how smart they are; remember a leader without followers isn't a leader. Theology needs us to work together. As Gricel and I argue throughout this book, theology must never be done alone. But learning to work as a team might be the hardest lesson a writer will need to master. Teamwork requires patience, the ability to compromise, and the skill to see your own weaknesses and shortcomings. Keep yourself among creative people who will nourish you and not nourish your fear or negativity. This isn't easy.

As dissertation writers, master many ways of knowing and break as many rules as possible. Writer Arthur Plotnik notes that "the unwritten rules of academic writing . . . decree a diction characterized by complex constructions, cautious vocabulary, and passive-voice dryness. One can buck the model, but at the risk of losing credibility and peer status."[3] If you are worried about your status, theology isn't the field for you. Speak up and speak out. As theologian Richard Lischer argues, theologians need to "remove the Bible from its native habitat in the church's worship, catechesis, and pastoral care . . . [and] take it out of the only world in which it has a chance to make sense."[4] Theology moves our faith into action. Dissertation writers need to allow readers to see beyond our current state and condition.

I believe the key to actually finishing your dissertation is love. You need to fall deeply, passionately in love with your work or you will never finish. Writing a dissertation can be a fairly desperate and lonely process. Write with passion or your dissertation will go nowhere. Remember, nobody cares unless you do. Many dissertation writers never know where to start or where they are going. Indeed, many never go anywhere, at least not on the page. Don't listen to the voices of doubt in your head. As a dissertation writer, your worst enemy is not a committee member out to get you; it's yourself. Your fears, doubts, anxieties, guilt. That little voice in your head

2. Lanham, *Revising Prose*, 114.

3. Plotnik, *Spunk & Bit*, 55–56.

4. Lischer, *The End of Words*, 53.

whispering, "I am not good enough." These are your enemies. Face them. Whether facing them requires therapy, spiritual companionship, or weekly pep talks from your support group, find what you need to do and do it. Falling in puppy love with your subject becomes the first step. But falling in love with your subject is not enough. You must build a foundation for your marriage to this subject. This is a long-term commitment. It will require communication, hard work, tears, and maybe even some counseling along the way.

Dissertations can become road blocks to actually becoming an author. Many writers develop some very bad writing habits while writing their dissertations. The habits you form by engaging your sources and crafting your prose in your dissertation can last a lifetime. You can write brilliant theology, but that doesn't make it well written. Write engaged, compelling, and beautiful prose in your dissertation. There is no rule against it. It might seem that dissertations are required to rely on dry, lifeless prose, but I have never discovered a dissertation manual at any university that makes this a rule.

Dissertation writing feels like a long process. Approach writing a dissertation like preparing for running a marathon. If you run a dissertation as a sprint, you will never see the finish line. Equip yourself for the journey—intellectually, emotionally, physically, and spiritually. Keep yourself whole during the process. I suggest creating a dissertation writing plan that includes objectives to keep yourself intellectually, emotionally, physically, and spiritually whole and charged. Eating healthy food, exercise, seeing your friends and family, reading exciting novels, and keeping yourself in contact with your community of faith and God provide more keys to a great dissertation than anything in a library. When any one of these factors weakens, your entire dissertation writing process suffers. Dissertation work can be brutal, but you have friends, including some you may have never met, cheering you on every day.

Read dissertations. Read lots and lots of dissertations. Reading dissertations always made me feel better about my writing. A good dissertation on a related topic will save you hours of research—that author has already mapped the way for you. A bad dissertation can also be a pick-me-up. When you find a terrible dissertation, remember that the author already earned a degree. You can do better.

As you write, I recommend sharing your work without fear. There are many potential road blocks to finishing your dissertation, but most of them begin with you. Most of our reasons for not sharing are lies. Mainly, we find reasons not to share because of our own fears. What if it isn't good enough? What if it makes me sound stupid? What if? What if? What if? But I ask you, what if not sharing keeps you from finishing? Remember all your work, all your money, and your investment. Being fearless means putting your draft chapters out into the open. It means putting them in the hands of readers and exposing all your weaknesses. Don't be afraid of readers finding mistakes and giving you corrections. If your chapter looks like a massacre when you get it back, remember it is one step closer to being done. And the best dissertation is a finished dissertation.

As a writer of theology, don't build your work on negativity. We can choose whether to make space for our work by tearing down another author's or by building on their foundation. Whole academic careers have been built on the shreds of other researchers' methods, discrediting the work of other writers, and pointing shortcomings in everyone else's studies. But theologians need to hold themselves to a higher ethical standard. We can frame our critiques to build a stronger approach, not to hide problems.

Focus. Remember you are writing theology. Find the center of hope in your message and cling to it. Write every day. One word after another, one page after another, and one chapter after another, until everything that you need to say is right there in front of you. Keep going. Don't stop for perfection, don't stop writing. An unfinished dissertation is likely to remain unfinished.

A friend of mine, Dr. Ted Whapham, always reminds people that a PhD is only a learner's permit. Don't believe you know everything about everything just because of a piece of paper. Keep learning, keep reading, and keep attempting to write engaged, compelling, and beautiful theology every day.

Finally: *keep your feet on the ground*

six

Beautiful Theology: The Craft

Once upon a time, my wife told a Confucian parable during her sermon at our home church in Miami, Florida. In this parable, Confucius stands next to a lake teaching his students. As he teaches, the sun sets in the west and a full moon rises in the east filling the sky above the lake with a golden light. Awed by its beauty, Confucius falls silent and raises his hand to point toward the moon. The students look at his pointing finger and question what it signifies. As Confucius stands there in silence, admiring the moon, the students debate their teacher's point. What is so important about his finger, they ask. They completely miss what that finger is pointing at. In the words of my wife, "That must have been one big, fat finger."

This parable and my wife's telling of it have stuck in my mind for over three years. Writers craft beautiful theology. It isn't born beautiful. We must help our readers understand our message. Readers must be empowered to see that beautiful golden moon. Often theological prose is born ugly: red, wrinkly, and crying out for help. Readers often miss our points because our big, fat fingers distract them. Only you, the one who imagined it into being, can see its potential beauty. Beautiful prose guides readers to our themes with loving care. Beautiful theological prose flows as simple, conversational writing that blooms with incredibly deep, complex ideas. It opens possibilities rather than restricting meaning. Each image, metaphor, and story seamlessly points towards the message. As Francine Du Plessix Gray argues, each element of a piece must "communicate, with eerie immediacy, the pitch of the author's central theme."[1] Beautiful theological prose sounds like a symphony where each note illuminates the theme.

1. Gray, "The Seduction of the Text," 6.

Writing beautiful theological prose doesn't hide the pain and ugliness of life. It captures life in all its ugliness and reveals the totality of it. As novelist Ernest Hemingway writes, "you can't do this without putting in the bad and the ugly as well as what is beautiful. Because if it is all beautiful you can't believe in it. Things aren't that way. It is only by showing both sides—3 dimensions and if possible 4 that you can write."[2] Beautiful prose exposes the reality of life with passion and clarity.

For me, beautiful prose demonstrates clear ideas in an elegant and passionate style that evokes the spoken word. But spoken, conversational language wanders all over the place. The beautifully written word takes the passion of the spoken word and reels it into an elegant flowing narrative that guides the reader inward to the heart of the idea without losing readers along the way.

TAKE A MOMENT TO REFLECT

1. What is beautiful prose for you? Is beauty in the eye of the beholder?

2. Remember what I recommend in chapter 4 about writing for your younger self and answer my question: what is beautiful prose for you?

You arrive at beautiful theology through hard work. Revision is a method not a mystical rite.[3] Crating beautiful prose means addressing your language and how you express it through words, sentences, and paragraphs in an authentic voice and style. To write beautiful theological prose, you have to understand language and your usage of it.

Language

Languages are living, breathing entities. Activist and writer Gloria Anzaldúa declares: "I am my language. Until I take pride in my language, I cannot take pride in myself."[4] As writers of theology, we must take pride in our language. Our words are shaped by our locations and experiences. We

2. Hemingway, *Ernest Hemingway on Writing*, 33.

3. Lanham, *Revising Prose*, iv.

4. Anzaldúa, *Borderlands La Frontera*, 81.

speak with accents and unique patterns shaped by life, culture, family, and more. For writers who engage English as a second language, there exists the underlying grammar of their native tongue. But no matter how many flaws and weaknesses we perceive in our writing, we need to take pride in our craft and build beautiful prose that welcomes readers. Words, sentences, paragraphs created with style and voice and personality take our readers by the hand and journey with them into the narrative. As we gaze upon our words, we should feel pride for our hard work, blood, sweat, and tears. Our writing doesn't need to be uniform; the realities of who we are and have been should always be part of our words. Don't try to make your language into the false idol of standard American or British English. Take pride in exploring the linguistic gifts God gives you.

This doesn't mean that we as writers don't need to master the basics of writing and grammar; rather, it means that we don't need to fit within someone's box of "perfect" linguistic expression. Beautiful language reflects its writer. You should see yourselves in your writing: your experiences, your expressions, and all the little, oddball linguistic patterns that shape you. Lynn Nelson explains, "that language is a mystery and a miracle that has been given to us we know not why."[5] We have the gift of language, and we must use it. Beautiful prose should reflect your spoken language without the sluggish hesitations and rambling babble of speak.

Writers of beautiful language do need to understand grammar, syntax, diction, and usage. If we (the writer and the reader) don't share similar boundaries of grammar, syntax, usage, mechanics, and diction, communication falters. We don't have to speak and write in the same voice, but our written language needs to share similar boundaries to effectively reach our audience.

Novelist James Michener, whose very long and detailed novels helped me survive middle school, argues that the writer must "first, learn to master the English sentence in all its richness of expression and variation in structure."[6] Mastering the English sentence stands at the starting point for beautiful theology. Writers can still express themselves in their own accents with their expressions and unique characteristics while sharing enough of the conventions of written English to communicate with their readers.

The main way writers maintain their linguistic uniqueness grows out of their diction (also known as vocabulary) and writing patterns. Theologian

5. Nelson, *Writing and Being*, 10.
6. Michener, "How to Identify and Nurture Young Writers," 29.

Thomas Merton believes that "if the artist, the peasant, the scientist, and the workman are all going to communicate together, their language will have to have a certain simplicity and austerity in order to be clear to them all without degrading thought."[7] Beautiful theological language must reach its intended audience with a shared vocabulary. This doesn't mean that you can't use big words now and then. It means that when you use vocabulary outside of everyday language, you need to unpack the word's meaning for your readers. You can't just drop pompous prose and expect to be understood. Your objective is to communicate, and this requires you to not confuse your readers. Starting in grade school, teachers reward students for using big words. But there is nothing wrong with one and two syllable words. This doesn't mean we, as theologians, are dumbing it down. It means that we are finding the best language to communicate with our intended audience. English is a huge and rich language. Don't shoot sentences full of steroids (big words, complex constructions, and strings of extra words) just to sound smart. Use the most common word to convey your point.

Vocabulary provides the staple of writing but don't write with a dictionary. Let your vocabulary grow, organically with experience. Every time you do something new, you add new words to your vocabulary. This is organic growth at its best.

I allow my language to flow out as a stream of consciousness onto the page. Then I begin to look for patterns and structure. I form my language into coherent groupings and begin to shape sentences. You, as a writer, have to have faith in your concepts and your ability to communicate them in your own language. You must believe you can create something beautiful on your terms.

Sentences

Annie Dillard tells this story: "a well-known writer got collared by a university student who asked, 'Do you think I could be a writer?' 'Well,' the writer said, 'I don't know . . . Do you like sentences?'"[8] When I read that last question, I stopped. "Do you like sentences?" The idea disrupted my train of thought. Dillard, the 1975 Pulitzer Prize winner for *Pilgrim at Tinker Creek,* fashions beautiful English sentences. She forces me to consider the power

---

7. Merton, *Echoing Silence,* 65.

8. Dillard, *The Writing Life,* 70.

of a sentence. For writers, sentences form the foundation of meaning. They are our medium for expression.

Many people believe words are more important than sentences, but anyone can vomit words onto a page. Individual words are meaningless without the order and structure of a sentence. For example, "pit cute know kitten," means nothing to a reader. Individual words without order or structure are meaningless. Good sentences remain hard to define, but bad sentences are easy to identify. A bad sentence is any sentence that a reader needs to read twice, not because the ideas are amazing or the concepts are thought provoking, but because the reader doesn't understand what the writer means.

Good sentences get right to the point. They illuminate rather than leave their readers in the dark. Often, long sentences seem to have been written by authors who wish to hinder more than enlighten. Now it's time: boil it down. Get to the point. Unlearn old habits. Graduate. And stop writing like an elementary school student. Find the heart of your message and give the reader what they need. Look at your sentences. When you discover one that takes more than three lines, check it. Has it gotten lost on the way to the dance? Two or three short sentences can drive a point home with more punch than one long sentence.

But what if you don't want to get right to the point? What if you want to build suspense or draw readers deeper into the narrative? Long sentences, or as Roy Clark calls them "*journey sentences*—create a flow that carries the reader down a stream of understanding."[9] Ask yourself: Does a long, streaming sentence convey the theme better? If it does, go with the flow, but keep your subject and verb close. It'll make your meaning easier to understand. Also, vary your sentence length to change the pace of your writing and allow your reader to pause and reflect. Give them a break; it's like taking a breather during a hard climb.

Good sentences are like a stairwell. Each step takes the reader closer to their destination. Each step adds one more concept to the argument, leading your reader on until they get to the top and see the big picture. Take care that one step leads to the next or your reader will stumble and fall if your ideas go off in a different direction, losing sight of your argument. Good sentences relate to those that came before and those that come after, taking the reader on a climb that takes them higher one idea at a time.

9. Clark, *Writing Tools*, 88.

Good sentences also tend to be active not passive. When writers write in the passive voice, they tell their readers that the action is not important. Let your readers know where the action happens. Make it clear who is doing the kicking. Active voice, according to Constance Hale, is "when the subject performs the action, and the passive voice, when the subject is or was acted upon."[10] This does not mean you will not find a use for passive voice sentences, or sentences where you place the subject and verb near the end. Writer Roy Clark notes, "if a writer wants to create suspense, or build tension, or make the reader wait and wonder, or join a journey of discovery, or hold for dear life, he can save subject and verb of the main clause until later. As I just did."[11] The intentional passive voice portrays passivity and places focus on the actor's lack of action. The placement of the subject and verb near the end of the sentence offers readers a chance to sight-see. When you want to portray the subject as being dominated and not in control use the passive voice. The occasional passive sentence can also break up your writing pattern and prevent choppiness.

Good sentences are not choppy. Choppy sentences make readers feel like they're sailing on a choppy sea of words; the constant pattern will make them sick and wear them down. When you get seasick it isn't from the occasional big wave; rather, the repetitive up and down, up and down, up and down, up and down. The same motion over and over. The same pattern again and again. The same swaying moving action back and forth. This sameness turns stomachs inside out. This is where sentence variety comes in handy; it keeps your readers from being hit by the same wave of words over and over again. Try reversing the order of a sentence now and then, or add a fresh word or phrase; stop the tedious motion of sameness. A little variety prevents sentence sickness.

There are four types of sentences: simple, complex, compound, and compound complex. Use them. The strongest of these is the simple sentence. Don't be thrown off by its humble style. Simple doesn't mean short but many are. It doesn't mean dumb. Simple sentences can be long, but their beauty lies in their ability to convey a strong, easy-to-follow message. Simple sentences make things clear. Roy Clark suggests "the next time you struggle with a sentence, rewrite it by placing subject and verb at the beginning."[12] A simple, declarative sentence captures a reader with one idea

---

10. Hale, *Vex, Hex, Smash, Smooch*, 155.

11. Clark, *Writing Tools*, 13.

12. Ibid., 14.

at a time—it's bite-sized, but full of flavor. Try to make a sentence do too much and you'll get into trouble. Your ideas will be too large for your reader to savor. Don't be afraid to break a long sentence into two or even three short ones to get your point across. Also don't be afraid to build a long simple sentence. But if multiple clauses and phrases start to sneak in, start adding periods.

The trick to producing good sentences is word order. First, when writers allow subjects and verbs to be separated by too many complex clauses, readers get lost. Again, remember good sentences keep subjects and verbs together. Second, good sentences make the most of words, putting the most important words at the beginning or end to make them stand out. They shout at the reader: "look at this!"[13] Third, they use parallel grammatical forms, adding a twist at the end to snap the reader to attention. This technique builds suspense. For example: faith, hope, and a cherry-red Ferrari I love; win, lose, or change the rules of the game; government of the people, by the people, with a turtle in charge.

Writers can engage lots of techniques to grow good sentences. Play with your words. If it doesn't work, your readers will tell you. But if it does work, you've struck gold. As a writer of beautiful theology, you must put each element of each sentence on trial.[14] Joy Sawyer argues that all a theologian needs is "to begin with one sentence, one melody line, a few lines of a pencil drawing. Such are the fragments where the frontier of beauty begin."[15] As a writer frames ideas in a sentence, a theology is born through the structure and meaning of language. When we get the basic architecture of the English sentence straight, everything else will follow.[16] One good sentence begins a pilgrimage. You construct these beautiful sentences from words, so that is what we explore next.

Take a Moment to Reflect

1. Do you have a favorite sentence?

2. What is a bad sentence for you?

---

13. Ibid., 15.

14. Prose, *Reading like a Writer*, 3.

15. Sawyer, *The Art of the Soul*, 13.

16. Lanham, *Revising Prose*, vii.

Words

Words matter. Words are not merely the writer's raw material. They provide the engine parts that make your sentence run. If all your parts are purring, your engine runs smoothly as you race towards successful communication. Every word must be important. For unimportant words, see the section entitled: Cut, Cut, and then Cut. As theologian Robert Jacks argues "we need to weigh our words carefully. Even tiny little pronouns can make a huge difference in whether or not the Word of God goes forth from our lips to *receptive* ears."[17] If one word makes your sentence falter, the whole statement will shake, rattle, and roll to a halt like an engine in need of a tune-up.

I believe writers must engage two key concepts: precision and clarity. Precision ensures that every word you use means what you intend it to mean. Is the word accurate? Clarity means not confusing your readers. Is the meaning clear to the reader? You need to make sure that everything matches: "your audience, your intention, your words."[18] Find the right words for the right audience and allow your message to grow in readers' minds.

Theologians must engage their word choice. Don't commit the sin of jargon. Jargon reeks of insider language. Jargon encapsulates the horizon of soteriological processes encircled by the *memoria passionis, mortis, et resurrectionis Jesu Christi* and embedded by the *Sitz im Leben* of the here and hereafter eschatology. Are you still with me? Sentences like that have been known to cause nose bleeds and ontological vertigo. Kathleen Norris tells readers, "when I began attending church again after twenty years away, I felt bombarded by the vocabulary of the Christian church. Words such as 'Christ,' 'heresy,' 'repentance,' and 'salvation' seemed dauntingly abstract to me, even vaguely threatening."[19] Not only do these words have loaded meaning within the language of faith, they also might have localized meaning within a local church or particular denomination. When a Roman Catholic uses the word "deacon," does it have the same meaning as when a National Convention Baptist uses the term? Jargon leaves outsiders in the dark. You want to bring people into the light of beautiful clear words.

Even beyond jargon, the language of faith is an insider language. You can confuse readers with our everyday theological lingo. Don't allow your

17. Jacks, *Just Say the Word!*, 43.
18. Ibid., 92.
19. Norris, *Amazing Grace*, 2.

words to become, as Robert Jacks calls them, "theological cotton candy floating over the heads of the congregation and never touching down into reality."[20] Use these words, but keep their feet on the ground. Explain them, illustrate them with examples, and unpack them for your readers.

Writers must also address the sin of wordiness. Words grow like weeds. They can overtake our beautiful word gardens and leave an overgrown mess. I recently read a government report that uses "long-term non-religious fasting" instead of "hunger strike." That is wordiness. Wordiness also always uses the big word instead of the short word, and adds adjectives and adverbs all over the place. Wordiness is a room decorated to death. William Strunk Jr. and E. B. White, in the classic book on writing *Elements of Style*, remind writers that "rich, ornate prose is hard to digest, generally unwholesome, and sometimes nauseating."[21] Clear, concise words empower readers. Don't use a pompous word when an everyday word suffices.

Look for patterns in your words. How do these words feel? How do they work together? Find words that you are overusing and replace them, but don't write with a thesaurus open on your lap. Don't be afraid to use words that readers probably weren't expecting. Find relational, conversational, encountering, communicating, communion building, colorful, and concrete words and sew them together into sentences.

English is a word rich language. Most dictionaries contain between 315,000 and 600,000 words total. [22] Author Constance Hale explains, "English is not only a mutt, it's a hungry mutt, scarfing up lively words from all corners." This offers writers many very precise words.[23] We collected words from French, Latin, and dozens of other languages, and are constantly coining new ones. This provides a deep well for writers to draw upon. You can craft new words, you can give a familiar word a new slant that reinvents its meaning,[24] and you can invent new words. Theologians love to invent new words or change the meaning of existing words without telling the reader. Feel free to invent or change, but give your readers a definition, or enough context to make sense of your usage. Don't drive your readers crazy with guessing. As Constance Hale argues, you can "experiment. Be dangerous. Play with words, mixing the curt with the lofty. Play with chains of words.

20. Jacks, *Just Say the Word!*, 124.

21. Strunk and White, *The Elements of Style*, 72.

22. Hale, *Vex, Hex, Smash, Smooch*, 12.

23. Ibid., 70.

24. Prose, *Reading like a Writer*, 26.

Play with phrases and clauses and dashes and full stops. Mix short with long, neat with nasty."[25]

Each word you place on the page represents a choice. Words are multidimensional; so these decisions are important. Words have their own denotation and connotation. Denotation refers to a word's literal meaning, as found in a dictionary, while connotation refers to the suggestive power of a word or its latent meanings.[26] Don't drop a word into a sentence without considering the ramification of your decision. Let beauty guide your word choice. Does the word sound good? Does it look good? Does it advance the message? Does it work for your audience? Does your word have the right moves?

TAKE A MOMENT TO REFLECT

1. What is your favorite word?
2. Have you discovered a new word recently?

Parts of Speech

As you consider your word choice, consider what each word does. The eight parts of speech are nouns, pronouns, adjectives, verbs, adverbs, conjunctions, prepositions, and interjections. Beautiful prose focuses on nouns and verbs. Too many adjectives, adverbs, and prepositions overwhelm your message. Give your reader concrete nouns and active verbs, and you are cooking with fire. Words furnish your building blocks, and nouns and verbs serve as the foundation.

Concrete nouns give more information than vague nouns. Don't forget my argument about concrete language from the last chapter. I hope you've blocked it out already. A vague noun often leaves the reader with an incomplete picture. Be specific: "cruising in a Ford Mustang" means more than "driving a car," and "fine dining on Cheerios" gives the reader more insights than "eating cereal." Concrete nouns conjure up precise images in the

---

25. Hale, *Sin and Syntax*, 151.
26. Ibid., 1–2.

minds' of readers.[27] When readers can visualize our words in their heads, ideas stick. Give them concrete nouns to paint a picture in their minds.

Like a great pairing of wine and cheese, you will need a powerful verb to go with your concrete noun. Nothing happens without a verb. Beautiful theological prose hungers for dynamic verbs. Take for example: cries, sobs, and weeps. Each of these verbs provides dynamic action but each also carries a different connotational twist. Find the best action verb for your sentence. Much of modern academic prose overflows with passive, wimpy verbs. Passive verbs are just happy to be. They fail to become anything special. Verb expert Constance Hale explains, "active verbs push hard; passive verbs tug fitfully. Active verbs also enable us to visualize an activity because they require a pronoun ('he'), or a noun ('the boy'), or a person ('Mrs. Scott') to put them in motion."[28] Give your readers action. Don't make your text so action-free that it feels like watching ancient, arthritic, great-grandfather tortoises race for a grape.

To rid your prose of weak verbs, remove forms of the verb "to be" whenever possible.[29] "To be" exists in many forms: am, is, was, were, be, being, and been. This verb drains the energy out of your party. For example: have been weeping, will have been crying, or should have been sobbing. Note how the compound "to be" verb steals the edge off the action. When all the other verbs hop onto the dance floor, your "to be's" are sitting around sipping tepid tap water. You will find many forms of the "to be" verb sitting there as compound verbs. Try to cut down on linking verbs and helping verbs that don't beef up your writing. If you can squeeze a compound verb hard,[30] often you find a simple action verb waiting to happen.

I recommend writers go through their work and circle every occurrence of the "to be" verb. If your page looks like a shooting target punched full of holes, you have a problem. To make them go away, look for the action and make that your verb. Not all "to be" verbs grow up to become bad influences on your sentences. Passive to-be verbs in passive sentences are perfect for wimpy passive characters; for example, read Hamlet's "to be or not to be" soliloquy. A perfect speech for a wimp. But unless the passive verb drives home your point, cut them. When you cut out weak verbs, beautiful prose blooms with simple, direct verb tenses.

27. Hale, *Vex, Hex, Smash, Smooch*, 33.

28. Zinsser, *On Writing Well*, 68.

29. Jacks, *Just Say the Word!*, 31.

30. Lanham, *Revising Prose*, 13.

English contains twelve different verb tenses. Theses tenses add a sense of time to your actions. As Constance Hall explains, "the simple tenses tell whether something *happens, happened,* or *will happen.*"[31] These simple tenses are past, present, and future, but English also contains progressive tenses, perfect tenses, and even the perfect progressive tense. Tense allows you to create a past perfect progressive verb. Writing with a simple, direct, past, or present tense produces happy readers and strong, healthy sentences. When picking a tense, ask yourself what makes it easier for the reader to follow? Pick the verb that enhances your style and intention. And watch out for shifting verb tenses. When someone "is seeking," "seeks," and "has been sought" all in the same narrative, your readers lose all sense of what is happening. It's not pretty.

Verbs energize your writing. Find the best verb to make your point. For example: listening and eavesdropping convey different actions and implications. Experiment with your verbs. Try an old verb in a new way or using a new verb like to google, to tweet, to friend, or to verb.

As for the other major parts of speech—adverbs, adjectives, and prepositions—make sure they do their own work in your sentences. As Constance Hale argues, you should "avoid using adverbs that merely repeat what the verb has already expressed: circle *around,* expedite *quickly,* merge *together.*"[32] Bad adverbs don't add anything new to the verb. Good adverbs add a twist to the verb that wasn't there before.[33] Does your adverb modify the verb, or does it just intensify it? Keep the adverbs that modify meaning and cut those that just intensify meaning. As for adjectives and prepositions, only add them when they express critical details. Remember every element needs to advance your message. Excessive adjectives give the reader too much to consider, and long chains of prepositional phrases lead nowhere.

Paragraphs

After examining word choice and sentence design, step back to check your paragraphs. Writers compose good sentences with clear words, concrete nouns, and punchy verbs, building these sentences into paragraphs.

31. Hale, *Vex, Hex, Smash, Smooch,* 131.
32. Ibid., 76.
33. Clark, *Writing Tools,* 29.

Paragraphs map your intent,[34] each representing another step on your journey. Let's return to our stairs metaphor; paragraphs are flights of stairs that take readers up or down. The first sentence of each paragraph should offer a direction for reading the rest of the paragraph. Keep in mind that readers pay more attention to the first and last sentences of a paragraph than what comes in the middle.[35] So place your most important concepts first and build up from there. Stephen King argues that a "topic-sentence-followed-by-support-and-description insists that the writer organize his/her thoughts, and it also provides good insurance against wandering away from the topic."[36] Three to five good sentences come together to deliver one beautiful paragraph.

Paragraphs should flow into each other. The beginning of each paragraph signals that a new step in the development of the subject has been reached.[37] Each paragraph should build on the paragraph before it and lead into the one after it, offering new details or arguments to your narrative while developing a clear relationship between paragraphs. As William Zinsser argues "take special care with the last sentence of each paragraph—it's the crucial springboard to the next paragraph. Try to give that sentence an extra twist of humor or surprise, like the periodic 'snapper' in the routine of a stand-up comedian. Make the reader smile and you've got him for at least one more paragraph."[38] Those ancient, arthritic, great-grandfather tortoises just got to the grape at the same time.

Your paragraphs layout impacts your reader every time they turn a page. A paragraph's length catches the eye before it has a chance to sink into your reader's brain. Keep your paragraphs short. Short paragraphs create white space (aka silence) around your concepts and make them look inviting to the reader, whereas long blocks of text discourage a reader from even starting to read a page.[39] Look at your page. How do your paragraphs look? Are there paragraph breaks? Are they all the same length? Consider your intended audience. Long paragraphs leave more room for good ideas to get lost in the middle. If you have a dynamic idea, place it in a very short paragraph to make it jump out at your reader.

34. King, *On Writing*, 130.
35. Prose, *Reading like a Writer*, 76.
36. King, *On Writing*, 131.
37. Strunk and White, *The Elements of Style*, 16.
38. Zinsser, *On Writing Well*, 55.
39. Ibid., 79.

Just as your sentence structure needs variety, your paragraphs need it too. A building with only one type of staircase looks boring, so does writing that overuses a single paragraph style. Interesting designs include spiral staircases, grand, curving stairwells, ladders. Make the most of your paragraph structures to build steps and landings that add sweeping curves and railings to your writing.

Like words and sentences, writers of beautiful theology must be willing to sacrifice and revise whole paragraphs. Annie Dillard warns writers that "only when a paragraph's role in the context of the whole work is clear can the envisioning writer direct its complexity of detail to strengthen the work's end."[40] After you revise at the word and sentence level, take a step back and revise at the paragraph level. If you can rebuild it, make it stronger. If it makes your work stronger to cut it, cut and paste it into a "not used but has potential file." But don't just delete it.

TAKE A MOMENT TO REFLECT

1. What is the perfect paragraph?
2. Have you ever considered paragraphs? Why not?

Sounds and Shapes

Let's try an experiment. Download three different versions of the hymn "Amazing Grace" from your favorite music service. I chose versions by Andrea Bocelli, Aretha Franklin, and Johnny Cash. But you can pick your own and listen to them over and over. Now grab a copy of the King James Version of the Bible—not a modern translation—and read Psalm 23 and Ecclesiastes 3. Next, listen to a recording of Martin Luther King Jr.'s "I Have a Dream" speech. First, just listen to it, then read along as you listen a second time. Examine the shape, sound, and structure of each of these texts as you do this. What makes these words work? Why do they stick in readers' minds? Why do they endure? Consider the beat and rhythm of the words. How do they appeal to your ear? How do they invade your mind and stick?

Aim for your readers' ear. Be aware of sound. Sound is invisible but it breaks through closed doors and penetrates cement walls. Writers need

40. Dillard, *The Writing Life*, 16.

to consider sound and beat in everything they write. As Richard Lanham contends, "rhythmless, unemphatic prose always indicates something has gone wrong."[41] Sound is the pulse—heartbeat—of your writing. Without a beat, writing dies. Beautiful theological prose embraces sounds, structures, and beats. They make theology beautiful.

Theologian Robert Jacks notes "when you start trying to write for the ear and not for the eye, you're going to find yourself at odds with many of the rules you've been taught. And that's okay. . . . But you're probably not going to start doing that until you realize how what we write for the *eye* can often sound contrived, artificial, and sometimes downright pompous."[42] When you write for the ear, your sentences linger in the minds of your readers. People remember beautiful lines; great lines make readers get caught up in the flow and beat of your text and keep them reading and re-reading.

This process begins with sounds. Writer Constance Hale argues "beyond the sense of a word is its sensuousness: its sound, its cadence, its spirit. The sounds of *peach* and *mango* differ, letting you play in different ways with surrounding words. In turning a phrase, we want the words to build like a jazz riff, with the melodies of one word playing off the melodies of the others."[43] Theologians need to cultivate an ear for words. How do their sounds, associations, and interactions work to create a lasting impression on readers. This includes playing with assonance, rhyme, alliteration, onomatopoeia. Start by reading your words out loud, then listen to other people reading your words out loud. Does this sound work for your message? Words that need to convey grief should sound different from words that express joy.

Also, consider slang words. You will need to explain them and explore their connotations, but they might bring the right sound to your text. Constance Hale believes that you shouldn't "shun slang, especially when it's vivid and musical and fills the gaps in the lexicon."[44] Note how different "shun slang" sounds from "don't use slang" or "avoid slang expressions."

Two of my foster daughters taught me the value of sound and meaning. One day, as we were riding to the park, I asked about their use of the word "ghetto." They explained to me that "ghettoo" means un-cool, while

41. Lanham, *Revising Prose*, 35.
42. Jacks, *Just Say the Word!*, 19.
43. Hale, *Sin and Syntax*, 2.
44. Ibid., 5.

"ghettoe" means cool, hip, and trendy. I love the English language. I hope my use of this example is ghettoe. See, it's all about sound.

Even as you work with sounds, shape your structure. Look back at the examples from the beginning of this section: "Amazing Grace," Ecclesiastes 3, and "I Have a Dream." Examine their structures. These are masterpieces of architectural design. As Kathleen Norris observes "repetition as in a hymn such as 'Amazing Grace,' or the ballade form, in poetry, where although the refrain is the same from stanza to stanza, it conveys something different each time it is repeated because of what is in the lines that have come in between."[45] This is where we build patterns, create movements, instill feelings that grow strong with each repetition. This is not the same as redundancy. Redundancy is a waste of words. Redundancy occurs when the meaning of the phrase never changes; repetition constantly adds, twists, and remakes to evoke or provoke.

Even a detail as small as word order becomes critical. If you think order is not important, try reciting the four evangelists in this order: Luke, Mark, John, and Matthew.[46] Re-read King's speech. Listen to how he plays on the lyric "from every mountain side, let freedom ring" from the song "My Country, 'tis of Thee." Each repeating stanza builds on the earlier generalities of the "prodigious hills of New Hampshire" and "snowcapped Rockies of Colorado," to the specific details of "Stone Mountain of Georgia" and "Lookout Mountain of Tennessee," to the universal "from every village and every hamlet." Stop, and reflect upon the impact of this last word. Hamlet. Why not community? Why not suburb? Why not crossroads? What critical impact does this word make?

Embedded within the sounds and structures of these examples is the beat. Rhythm. When your writing plods on like a lame horse instead of running like a thoroughbred, you go nowhere fast. Francine Prose suggests that "rhythm is nearly as important in prose as it is in poetry."[47] You got to find your beat. You got to drum out your tempo. As Constance Hale explains "rhythm remains essentially beat—whether the 4/4 time of rhapsodies or the urgent tempo of rap. Rhythm is repetition, incantation, timing . . . that deep—down sense of music that is as inborn as a heat—beat."[48]

---

45. Norris, *Amazing Grace*, 64.

46. Clark, *Writing Tools*, 95.

47. Prose *Reading like a Writer*, 56.

48. Hale, *Sin and Syntax*, 243.

Keep asking yourself: does this cadence reinforce my message? Read your work out loud. Where do you stumble? Make your words sound beautiful.

Punctuation

Punctuation provides a key to a beautiful sound. I love Lynne Truss's example on the value of punctuation:

- A woman, without her man, is nothing.

- A woman: without her, man is nothing.[49]

How's that for changing the meaning of a sentence? Replace a comma with a colon, move another comma and the whole meaning shifts. Punctuation is amazing! Truss explains, "punctuation marks are the traffic signals of language: they tell us to slow down, notice this, take a detour, and stop."[50] Punctuation controls things like reading speed, patterns, how ideas merge. Punctuation marks tell readers how we, as writers, want them to interpret our sentences. If you believe punctuation is not important, try writing without it.

To write beautiful theological prose, writers need to understand punctuation and be ready to play with it. Break the rules if the sounds work. Bend them if it produces something intriguing. As theologian Robert Jacks contends "this isn't a call for grammatical anarchy. Writers need to know what's right, what's correct, and know why we're bending or breaking the rules."[51] But ask yourself: "what's the most natural way of saying this?"[52] Too little punctuation or too much punctuation? Either one can keep your theology from being beautiful.

---

49. Truss, *Eats, Shoots and Leaves*, 9.

50. Ibid., 98.

51. Jacks, *Just Say the Word!*, 47.

52. Ibid.

Cut, Cut, and then Cut

Now it is time to cut. Cut words, cut sentences, cut paragraphs, and cut sections. I know that cutting feels painful, but to find beautiful prose you need to cut. I agree with William Zinsser who believes that "clutter is the disease of American writing."[53] Ask yourself does this sentence or this word or whatever get my reader to the core message? Sometimes you want to be a meandering brook and other times you need to be a fast-flowing white-water rapid. But whatever style this project calls for, you must get your reader there without hitting dams or leaving them lost in a swamp.

I recommend attempting to cut 10 percent of your writing between the first and second draft. You are trying to distill your message. Novelist Ernest Hemingway recommends that you should be "boiling it down always, rather than spreading it out thin."[54] I enjoy this image, boiling it down. Whether you are making a sauce or distilling liquid, you want to give it a powerful kick without boiling your pot dry. Simplify, simplify. Leave out the buzz words; they're only filler.

Begin at the word level. Examine every word in the sentence. Is it necessary? If you put your finger over that word, does the sentence still make sense? Cut compound verbs; write in a simple past or present tense. You can also cut out most adjectives and adverbs without harm. Cut unneeded prepositional phrases. Many of your "that's" and "which's" can disappear. Now, go to the sentence level. Then to the paragraph level and the section level, what does each part do? Will your engine still run without these parts? Try it. Clean out the clutter and boil down the rest. When your reader reads a concise, compact message, they feel the kick. Love your subject not your words. It is hard to cut words you love. You must be ready and willing to kill them! Consider novelist George R. R. Martin's readiness to kill off beloved characters he spent hundreds of pages developing. Now that takes guts. If the element doesn't advance your message no matter how beautiful or insightful it is, it has to go bye-bye.

Role Models

After pondering your sentences, words, and paragraphs, consider your role models. You need good role models. If you want to write better theological

---

53. Zinsser, *On Writing Well*, 6.

54. Hemingway, *Ernest Hemingway on Writing*, 3.

prose, read good theological prose. Musicians, painters, and architects all have role models, masters who inspire them to create. Theologians need role models too. William Zinsser believes you need to "find the best writers in the fields that interest you and read their work aloud. Get their voice and their taste into your ear—their attitude toward language. Don't worry that by imitating them you'll lose your own voice and your own identity. Soon enough you will shed those skins and become who you are supposed to become."[55] After you find a role model, begin reading their work. Don't just read one book; read a shelf. Read materials they wrote at the beginning of their writing careers. Then pick up some works from their mid and later career. Sample the width and breadth of their genres and styles. Read their stories and their poetry as well as their non-fiction theological prose.

As you read their works out loud, as Zinsser suggests, explore their language, their words, their sentences, their paragraphs. What makes it beautiful? Why do you enjoy it? Let their writing be a mirror for helping you to understand what you like in beautiful theology. Lay out your writing next to theirs and look at the page. What is this master writing on the page that makes you love their writing? Go and do likewise. Don't copy their style and voice; rather, write in the same spirit. Don't be a mini-C. S. Songs or a mini-Rowan Williams or a mini-Thomas Merton or a mini-Barbara Brown Taylor; just be yourself as a writer-in-communion with your role model.

Austin Kleon suggests writers need to move beyond imitation to emulation. He writes "imitation is about copying. Emulation is when imitation goes one step further, breaking through into your own things."[56] Kleon engages the example of parents. You are neither your father nor your mother although you resemble both of them in some ways whether physically, emotionally, or intellectually. Just as you are a remix your ancestors, your writing reflects your roles models.[57] Write as a member of your role model's extended family. Reading a lot and writing a lot makes you a better writer, and reading beautiful theology empowers you to write beautiful theology.

55. Zinsser, *On Writing Well*, 235–36.
56. Kleon, *Steal like an Artist*, 38.
57. Ibid., 11.

1. Who do you want to emulate? Why?

Voice and Style

Your voice and style mature as you emulate your role models. I love the story of Jesus walking on water in the Gospel of Matthew. It goes like this.

While Jesus was praying up on a mountain, his disciples were sailing across the Dead Sea when a storm came up. The waves got high; the winds got strong. And the little boat started doing things you don't want your boat to do. Spinning, twisting, and jumping a jig across the waves. These disciples weren't some city slickers; they were hardcore fishermen. They knew the difference between a sprinkle of light raindrops and a gale. They knew trouble when they saw it. And this was trouble. A raging tempest. A life-threatening squall. This wasn't going to be some dancing in the rain experience. This was about them becoming fish food.

It was 3 am, pitch black except for the lightning cracking. Waves were battering the boat. Wind burned against their faces. And the disciples were beyond panicked. They were frozen in fear. Jesus was with them during other storms, and he took care of storms. Jesus was the one who stilled storms, who calmed waves, who rebuked the winds, but Jesus wasn't with them in that boat. Or was he? His disciples needed him, and Jesus was coming to them. He was coming to take care of them. He was coming to save them. They needed a miracle, and Jesus came walking across the waves to give them one.

But when the disciples saw Jesus, they became even more afraid. They thought they saw a ghost. But Jesus yelled out over the storm, "Don't worry; it's just me. I'm coming."

Peter was really scared—of the storm, the wind, the waves, the ghost. So Peter called out to Jesus, "Lord if it's you, tell me to come to you."

And Jesus called him. Peter took off running across the water, but then he remembered, "I can't walk on water," and began to sink. Jesus reached out and saved him. Then Jesus rebuked him.

Now the common reading of this passage is that Jesus is telling Peter that he wouldn't have started sinking if he had had more faith. The common reading here is that Jesus is telling us we can do anything if we have enough faith, even walk on water. But, my friends, what if Jesus was rebuking him for not having enough faith to stay in the boat? What if Jesus was rebuking him for not having enough faith to believe that he would be saved? What if Peter didn't have enough faith to let God do God's thing? Sometimes in our lives, it takes more faith to stay in the boat than it does to jump out and try to walk on water.

I want us to remember that walking on water is God's thing. Peter wants to do what God alone does. But it is God's thing to walk on water. We need to remember that no matter how great our faith is, we are not God. It is God's job to walk on water, it is God's job to heal, it is God's job to see the big picture. Sometimes God needs us to stay in the boat and sometimes God needs us to jump out and swim.

Notice that I chose to retell this story in my own voice and style instead of just quoting it to you from the Gospel of Matthew. Voice is your writing personality. And style is how you express it. It is not only what you write but how you write it. Your voice and style must be authentic. They are you. Beautiful theological prose requires you to be yourself. Stay in your boat. Let the message come to you. Don't fake it and try to walk on water. That's a God thing and you're not God.

Let your content and intended audience shape your voice and style. Theologian Richard Lischer argues "the text will tell you when to be angry, ironic, funny, or sad. It will tell you when to reason with your hearers and when to tease them with parabolic utterance, when to teach your parishioners in the synagogue and when to soar with them to the third heaven."[58] Funerals provide a great example of this. The deceased person's personality dictates the eulogy I write for them. Ironic practical jokers and dead-beat, violent drunks deserve very different words. Let the situation, the subject, the sources govern your voice and style. A writer's voice and style needs to mold itself to its content.

Also consider your audience. Poet John Leax reflects, "I chose a language held in common with my audience, and I consciously used the rhythms of spoken sentences to hold my thoughts. . . . My voice remains simple and direct, closely connected to speech."[59] This is great advice. Your voice and style need to fit your intended audience.

Finally, let your voice and style develop naturally. As the authors of *Elements of Style* recommend "a careful and honest writer does not need to

58. Lischer, *The End of Words*, 80.
59. Leax, *Grace is Where I Live*, 85.

worry about style. As you become proficient in the use of language, your style will emerge, because you yourself will emerge, and when this happens you will find it increasingly easy to break through the barriers that separate you from other minds."[60] It is a God thing to walk on water. Just stay in the boat, be yourself, and think about your content and your audience. Being ourselves should be all of our styles.

TAKE A MOMENT TO REFLECT

1. How would you describe you writing style?

Flow

Beautiful prose flows. It sounds natural, and your hard work, sweat, tears, and blood all seem to disappear behind your flowing narrative. Your narrative needs to grace the eyes and lodge naturally in the readers' minds, hearts, and souls. Two factors impact your narrative's flow more than anything else: headings/subheadings and your use of other people's words.

Headings and subheadings empower readers to enter and exit your narrative smoothly and without confusion. They work as exit and entrance ramps to and from the expressway of text. Headings create white spaces that serve as rest areas. They give readers a chance to process information, take a break, and find a natural re-entry point to return to the text. The art of headings requires you to design them. This means spacing them out, transitioning readers into and out of the text, and creating a logical order with great signage.

Begin with the logical ordering. How do your headings and subheadings relate to each other? Writers need to fashion a logical order that makes sense to readers. Each section needs to provide a logical transition to the next section. Each subheading needs to add something new but still related to its heading. Play with the order. Try moving sections. Ask the readers who help you during the editing and revision stages to reflect on the ordering of headings and subheadings. Then examine the words in the heading. Do these words give a clear sense of the upcoming text? The words in a

---

60. Strunk and White, *The Elements of Style*, 70.

heading provide the signage that directs the readers. It gives them a heads-up, a foretaste, a warning.

Proceed to the spacing between each heading. Too long and readers will take unintended breaks. Too little and readers will find too many excuses to walk away. Balance. Balance. And then balance some more. The final element in making sections flow requires writers to manage the sentences that come right before and after a heading. These transition sentences move readers out of one topic and into another. They provide closure and welcome. They remind readers where they have been and where they are going. Remember headings and subheadings are an art. With practice, any writer can master them.

Your use of quoted and paraphrased material is also critical to the smooth flow of beautiful narrative. As a reader, nothing feels worse than hitting the white water rapids of a bad quote. Bad quotes, too many quotes, and misleading quotes all stop readers. To prevent this, make sure that the quotations you pull agree with the point you are making. Secondly, don't let the other writer's voice overwhelm your own. Just because you collected all this great research doesn't mean you have to use it.[61] I know it is tempting. I keep a file for each of my writing projects called: great stuff/not used. For this book, I have over one-hundred pages of funny, insightful, and wise quotes from over thirty authors in my great stuff/not used file.

Select the quotes that will make your narrative more beautiful, more compelling, and more engaging. Be inspired. Pour a little of this author and some of that author into the blender of your mind. Mix, mash, and discover. If you find critical quotes, but their writing style falls flat and breaks up the flow of your own writing, paraphrase and credit the original source behind your inspiration.[62] Don't forget the Ten Commandments, especially the one on theft. Correlate your quotes, your paraphrasing, and your ideas in ways that are both faithful and creative. Let it flow.

Conclusion

Theological prose isn't born beautiful but with our hard work, sweat, and tears as dedicated authors, it can grow-up into something beautiful. In the next chapter, Gricel Dominguez empowers theologians to make their prose beautiful through the processes of revising and editing.

61. Jacks, *Just Say the Word!*, 39.
62. Hale, *Vex, Hex, Smash, Smooch*, 118.

seven

Beautiful Theology

Editing and Revising, Taking it to the Next Stage

Advice from a Writing Nerd

We'll be taking a break from our regularly scheduled program. . . . Until this point, you've received advice on improving your work as a theological writer, now I'm going to give you advice from a writer's perspective. This chapter is based on strategies used to edit both academic prose and creative writing, as well as techniques used in introductory composition classes to introduce students to the writing process.

The methods described here are not one-size-fits-all, but they are easy to follow and can help you find your own best practices. There is no right or wrong way to edit and revise writing; the only rule is that you come to the page with an open mind and accept the challenge to read your work and commit to (re)writing the best piece you can produce. But first, a couple of pointers to recall when thinking about revision vs. editing: think of revision as the real work that goes into polishing your writing, it's the part that takes the most time and energy, but will have the greatest impact on your writing. Editing, on the other hand, happens throughout the revision process, but especially after full-scale revision. Editing is where you get down to the nitty-gritty details.

The Sweet Torture of Reading Your Own Writing

You've written your essay/chapter/letter/email . . . whatever form your writing takes; the process doesn't end when you jot or type that final period. Writing is a messy affair. It can lead you on a powerful rollercoaster ride of emotion, but nothing is more dreaded than the task of reading our own words.

There is something intimate and unsettling about reading our own writing. It's a part of you. It bares your thoughts and cements them in a way that conversation alone cannot achieve. The only thing worse than reading our own words is letting another read them.

Now, I'm going to ask you to do just that. Read your writing. Share it. Learn from it. And get ready to make it shine.

Polishing and Revising Your Work

By now you've established your writing process. You've identified your audience and purpose, you've started discovering your voice as a writer, and you've done your research. You've put it all together into a piece of writing that you're proud of—whether it took you hours or weeks to write, you finished what you set out to do. Congratulations! Now, take a breather, grab a cuppa, and get ready for the real work.

Writing without revising is like baking a cake and forgetting to add the final layer of frosting before serving—it may look ready to eat, but you know something's missing and your reader will too. Revising is difficult, but your audience will thank you for it. This chapter will discuss tips and tricks for improving your writing, managing your revisions, and making the most of your work by taking the time to read, revise, rewrite, and recruit helpful readers.

Why Bother Revising?

There is more to revision than a quick spell-check or proofread for misspellings. Real revision takes time and often requires more than one round. To understand revision, it's important to recognize what it is not.

1. Revision is not reading for spelling mistakes.

2. Revision is not a simple line edit.

3. Revision is not a one-step process.

Every writer can gain from the revision process by uncovering weaknesses in their style and prose, finding holes in their arguments, becoming better writers as they become critical readers of their own work. This book will have gone through several revisions before reaching your shelf. The more aware we are of our writing, the more likely we are to avoid making the same poor stylistic choice twice.

Think of your writing as a process that involves drafting, revision, and rewriting. Just as every piece of prose, poetry, or reflection takes you through a different thought-process and learning experience, how you revise will depend on your goals and intentions for each piece, so plan ahead and allow yourself ample time to allow your work to reach its full potential.

Many new and inexperienced writers avoid revision; often because they are convinced that their work is as good as it's going to get, or simply because they believe they cannot read their work critically in order to self-edit. Rarely is a piece so brilliantly crafted that it can do without revision, so don't do yourself and your readers the disservice of presenting them with a half-hearted effort. We can all learn to self-edit if we're willing to try. Revising your work requires that you put yourself in the role of reader—so sit down and read. However, before you do that, it's a good idea to give yourself some time away from your piece. Let it rest and marinate. Whether you plan on reading a digital or a hard copy, set it aside and don't look at it for at least a couple of days or weeks (this is where that time management comes in handy). It's best to not revise as soon as you finish writing; you need to be able to let your thoughts and ideas rest in order to return to your work with fresh eyes and an open mind. Distance will not only make your heart grow fonder, it will allow you to find the clarity you need to see your writing anew. When you come back to your work, you may find that lines that made perfect sense no longer work. The urgency to get your thoughts down before they fade can blind writers to the presence (or absence) of small details that can have a large impact on meaning and message.

Getting Started

After you've finished your draft and set it aside, it's time to start revising. There is no prescribed way to revise written work. Just as pre-writing and brainstorming are uniquely personal processes, so too is revision. The following is a rough guide to get you started on the road to developing your own personal strategies for revision. Think of these as guideposts—they can lead you on your journey, but it's okay to find your own way.

You want to write? You have to learn to let go.

The first step in rewriting is reading. Settle in and read your draft in its entirety. You may choose to read it on a screen or print a hardcopy, but whatever your preferred format, read with a critical eye. Read for content before you start getting down to word choice and sentence structure. Examine your writing closely: Do your paragraphs flow? Are your points well-researched and supported? Are there gaps in your reasoning? Inspect your work on a global level to identify areas that need to be refined or developed. Does each paragraph have a solid topic sentence and supporting details? A strong topic sentence not only tells the reader what the paragraph is about, it outlines the information that will follow. Use a colored pen or pencil to mark, circle, highlight, and annotate any areas that need to be revised, or use the comment feature on your word processor. If you're pressed for time, you can edit as you revise, making changes while marking areas that need a complete overhaul, but I recommend reading the complete draft before making sentence-level edits. As you read, you may find that some of your points need to be reorganized or reworded; there's no sense in making sentence level edits if entire sections need rewriting. Critically annotating your work will help you determine the best way to structure your piece so that it flows in a logical, coherent manner.

While working on structure, review your transitions. Many beginning writers find it difficult to determine how to use transitions to their advantage. There is a fine balance between using no transitions and using too many. Without transitions—those words and phrases that lead your reader from one point to the next—an essay can seem stilted and abrupt. Too many, and your essay reads like a how-to guide, taking your reader through a seeming list of instructions. Transitions should guide the reader without being obtrusive. They should come naturally into the text and create a connection between what came before and what will come after. Writing strong topic sentences that clearly outline the content of the paragraph or section will make it easier to write effective transitions. Consider this paragraph; I opened with the statement: "While working on structure, review your transitions." I could just as easily have written, "In addition, while working on structure, review your transitions." However, (see, another transition), I prefer the less formal version without the transition. Transitions are a matter of choice as much as style. There is no need to rely on the standard, eighth-grade list of transitions when writing; good sentence variety and a clear understanding of your subject and structure will help you make the best use of transitions.

WRITING TIP

Post-outline as you read your paper; this will help you visualize your arguments in a linear manner and reveal information that may be better suited in a different section of your work, or which can be cut to improve flow.

The next step in reading for content is reading for redundancy and irrelevance. Often we write *every* thought that comes into our minds, especially when we're on a deadline and under pressure. Some of these ideas are gems, but there are also plenty of doozies. Redundant information takes away from the experience of reading and makes your work seem longwinded and rambling. Reiterate important points, but avoid repetitive statements that fail to advance your argument or serve as filler. Mark up your page, cross them out, save what can be saved and move on. A good idea is to mark those points that might be worth salvaging. Learning to edit requires learning to let go. Many beginning writers feel that every word is precious. It was such a struggle to get them down in the first place; they're sacred, right? Wrong! If you aren't willing to let go, get out now, do not pass go.

Still there? Great. Now you're ready to start cutting. Create a separate file and save it as "Pieces," "Brainwaves," or whatever you like. Think of this as your idea dump; all those extra, messy pieces that don't quite fit will go into this file. If necessary, jot down a quick note to remind yourself why you think it might be salvageable. Keep this file open during the rewriting stage; it will help you let go of padding without losing anything of real value.

Getting Down to Details

You've read and annotated your draft, marking it up so much it looks like a murder scene (at least, that's what my first drafts usually look like); now it's time to move on to sentence-level editing. If you are editing in print, it's a good idea to take the time to apply any changes you've marked and print out a fresh copy. Save your draft under a new file name so you can return to an earlier version if you decide to restore previously deleted material (saving edited drafts as separate files will also help you visualize the process as your final draft unfolds).

Sentence-level editing, also known as local revision, is the kind of revision that involves editing for spelling, grammar, and sentence-level changes. Editing for word choice is also part of sentence-level editing, but don't get hung up on individual words; the best word is often the one that's already part of your vocabulary. A thesaurus is a great tool, but it's terribly easy for a well-written message to become ambiguous when a writer decides that the best word is the one that sounds "smarter." This is a common mistake that writing students make in an effort to sound informed. The result is often strange and convoluted. Stephen King discusses this in his memoir, *On Writing*, noting:

> One of the really bad things you can do to your writing is to dress up the vocabulary, looking for long words because you're maybe a little ashamed of your short ones. . . . Remember that the basic rule of vocabulary is *use the first word that comes to your mind, if it is appropriate and colorful.*[1]

When reading for sentence-level changes, focus on the message rather than the words. Is your meaning clear? Is the voice and style appropriate to the message? Do the individual sentences add up to a well-constructed paragraph? One that features a strong topic sentence followed by supporting statements that lead into the next paragraph? If so, you're on the right track.

In *Line by Line*, Cook suggests that while revising "you can think of your draft as a puzzle; to solve it, you have to find and eliminate the superfluities that obscure your meaning. The object is to delete as many words as possible without sacrificing stance or nuance."[2] Editing for grammar is simple—the rules of grammar haven't changed much since you learned the basics—but even if you can't identify the parts of speech, chances are you can construct a decent sentence. However, if your meaning is buried behind wordy, unclear, and awkwardly worded sentences, proper comma usage will make little difference.

While this chapter is not meant to serve as a grammar guide (there are plenty of well-written, easy-to-follow guides available in print and online), the following are some of my personal favorites. These guides provide easy

---

1. King, *On Writing*, 110.
2. Cook, *Line by Line*, 17.

to follow advice for new and experienced writers, and can serve as a quick reference when in doubt.

If you like your grammar with a side of humor, take a look at The Oatmeal's infographic guides: http://theoatmeal.com/tag/grammar

For a no-nonsense guide to better writing and how-to tips on everything from comma splices to verb usage, try Grammar Girl Mignon Fogarty's Quick and Dirty Tips: http://www.quickanddirtytips.com/grammar-girl

For a more academic approach to writing, try Purdue University's Online Writing Lab's guide to general writing strategies: https://owl.english.purdue.edu/owl/section/1/

For a list of print resources, see the recommended reading guide at the end of the book.

Finessing Your Style

If you've been following the advice outlined in this text, you've already determined the best style and voice for your intended audience. Several factors affect style, including tense, point of view, word choice, sentence variety, and more. Editing for style happens throughout the revision process as you review your writing and determine the best and most effective way to communicate with your readers. Nevertheless, revising with an eye towards style and voice is always recommended. When editing for style, start by looking for weak verbs. Are you writing in the active or passive voice? You can set your spell checker to identify instances where you rely on the passive voice if you're unsure how to spot them. Just remember: a sentence written in the passive voice is one in which the subject of the sentence is being acted *upon* rather than performing the action.

Warning: grammar-speak ahead.

A passive verb construction happens when you use a variation of *"to be"* + *the past participle of the main verb (or action).*

Mary was given [to be + verb] *an award by Lois.*

In this case, Mary is being acted upon. She "was given" an award.

It's actually quite easy to change a passive sentence to an active one by rewriting it so that the one performing the action becomes the subject of the sentence.

Lois [the actor] *gave* [verb] *Mary* [the one being acted upon] an *award.*

In this example, Lois is the one performing the action.

This is a very simplistic example, but by being aware of how passive voice sentences are constructed, it will become easier to recognize and avoid them in writing.

Also consider other ways in which word choice affects sentence structure. Are you using a string of weak words where one strong verb or descriptive noun will suffice? For instance, do you overuse phrases such as "due to the fact that" when a simple "because" will do? Are you padding your sentences with overblown metaphors and similes? A good writer makes use of all the tools available to craft their piece; recognizing when words are merely padding is part of being a good writer. Keep your sentences tight. Richard Palmer calls this "fighting the flab" and identifies this excess as "waffle and padding" to be avoided at all cost. A writer waffles "when they have nothing to say and/or no control over their material."[3] This kind of writing happens when you're uncomfortable or unfamiliar with your subject. The best way to avoid waffling is to do your research and be well-informed before writing. However, if you've already rambled your way through your essay, it's time to cut. Slash your way through unnecessary material and trim your piece down. Padding detracts from an otherwise well-structured, clear sentence. One word that is often littered throughout student essays is "basically." *Basically, the writer is arguing that the world is flat. My teacher is basically saying that my writing is no good.* Just ban it. It serves no purpose and interrupts the flow of your sentence.

3. Palmer, *Write in Style*, 63–64.

Similarly, tautologies—nerd speak for statements that combine more than one word with the same meaning—take away from your writing by padding sentences with unnecessary information. These can be effective in some contexts, but are best avoided in academic writing and other genres where a concise sentence structure is expected.

> For instance:
> *The incredibly tall skyscraper reached towards the clouds.*
> A skyscraper *is* incredibly tall, so your reader will make that connection without the extra words.
> *The skyscraper reached towards the clouds.*
> The meaning is the same, but the flab is gone. If you're writing with an audience in mind, trust your readers to understand your meaning without adding unnecessary details.

Read it Out

But what about the spelling and grammar, you ask? We're getting to that. Proper spelling and punctuation are an integral part of good writing, but they are *not* the key to good writing. Purpose, clarity, and personal style will do more for your writing than perfect spelling and grammar. Editing for spelling and grammar can happen throughout the rewriting process, but it's best to hold off on making these changes until the final draft so that you can catch any mistakes made while rewriting and revising.

As I noted previously, most writers are already familiar with the basic rules of writing, so there's no reason to be intimidated by commas, semicolons, and other forms of punctuation. If you're still in doubt, read your work aloud. There is a natural pattern to spoken English; when you read aloud, you fall into that pattern. Do you pause after an introductory clause? Add a comma. Is that pause somewhat longer than a beat? A semicolon will do you good. Does your sentence read like a breathless, nervous ramble? Sounds like a run-on to me. Read it again and note those natural beats. Punctuate accordingly.

Keep those Sentences in Check

Though I promised this wouldn't be a grammar guide, a chapter on editing wouldn't be complete without a refresher. Apologies in advance for the terrible dinner party examples; I too dislike explaining the rules. The following are some of the most common writing mistakes and offenses I've encountered in my years as a student, instructor, librarian, and writer. These are the ones that we've all made at least once (yes, I do mean *all* writers). Know how to find and fix these issues and you're on your way to improving your writing.

The Usual Suspects: A Line-Up of Common Writing Mistakes

Crimes against Punctuation

Commas

A lot of writers will fall into the trap of overusing commas (a comma splice) or not using them at all, resulting in a run-on sentence (see below). Think of commas as natural pauses; they separate items in a list, unite independent and dependent clauses, and mark introductory phrases.

Examples:

Independent + Dependent Clause

We enjoyed the meal, but found the conversation terribly boring.

"We enjoyed the meal" can stand on its own as a sentence, making it an *independent clause*. The second part, "found the conversation terribly boring" is a dependent clause because it can't survive as a standalone sentence. The two clauses are supported by a comma and a conjunction (but).

Items in a List

We enjoyed the meal, the wine, and the excellent music.

Each of these items can be turned into a complete sentence (We enjoyed the meal. We enjoyed the wine. We enjoyed the excellent music.), but the comma serves to bring them all together.

After an Introductory Word or Phrase

As night turned to morning, we said our goodbyes.

"As night turned to morning" serves as an introductory phrase, but it is dependent on the second part of the sentence. Introductory phrases also include transitions and can often be rearranged within a sentence.

Comma Misuse

A comma splice occurs when a writer uses a comma instead of a period or semicolon to join (or *splice*) two complete sentences into one.

We left the party after midnight, it was still going strong.

One of the best ways to find a comma splice is to read the sentence out loud. If it sounds stilted, it probably is. Best practice is to remove the comma and revise the sentence.

Examples:

Turn it into two sentences:

We left the party after midnight. It was still going strong.

Add a comma and coordinating conjunction:

We left the party after midnight, but it was still going strong.

Rewrite the sentence with the first part as an introductory phrase:

Though we left the party after midnight, it was still going strong.

Replace the comma with a semicolon:

We left the party after midnight; it was still going strong.

Semicolons

Semicolons are the wayward love-child of periods and commas. They unite independent clauses (two complete sentences), keep super lists in line, and mark transitions.

Examples:

Independent clause + Independent clause

There was an archaeologist at the party; she spent the night telling stories about her travels.

Each of these clauses can stand alone as a complete sentence:

There was an archaeologist at the party.

She spent the night telling stories about her travels.

When in doubt, read each part as an individual sentence. Can each half be read as a complete sentence with a verb and a predicate? If not, unite the pieces with a comma and/or a conjunction.

To manage long lists
Semicolons aid commas when creating lists within lists.

Example: *Our hostess served cheese, grapes, and cold ham; a salad and two kinds of soup; an elegant seafood dish with a side of fragrant rice and sauce; and three kinds of dessert.*

Each clause can easily be rewritten as a single sentence:

Our hostess served cheese, grapes, and cold ham.

Our hostess served a salad and two kinds of soup.

Our hostess served an elegant seafood dish that came with a side of fragrant rice and sauce.

Our hostess served three kinds of dessert.

However, by using semicolons to bring the pieces together into a single, multi-part, complex sentence, the statement becomes much more fluid and less clunky.

Colons

A well-placed colon can provide the right amount of emphasis when citing additional information or following up with a list. The information that comes after the colon is dependent on what came before it and directly related to it.

Example:

A colon is placed after a complete sentence: to create emphasis, make a point, or introduce a list that is directly related to the first part of the sentence.

Dashes

Dashes, not to be confused with hyphens, indicate an aside—the information is supplemental to the sentence, but not essential (they can also be used in place of parentheses so as not to disrupt the flow of a sentence).

Periods

By now, you know how periods work, but there are instances when you lose sight of your writing and forget to place a period at the end of a sentence. Like the occasional misspelling, periods can sometimes escape your notice. Don't rely on autocorrect to catch your mistakes; read and edit with care.

Runaway Sentences

Run-ons

Have you ever tried to make sense of the breathless, small-print statements at the end of car commercials? That's what a run-on reads like. It's a long string of thoughts, written without pause, and often combining more than one complete thought to create an over-long, convoluted, confusing statement.

Read your run-ons carefully, noting the natural pauses. Punctuate accordingly.

Fragments

Sometimes, writers forget . . . to finish their sentences. Fragments happen. They are incomplete sentences where either the subject or verb is missing. A fragment leaves your reader hanging. They can be used effectively to convey emotion in certain styles of writing, but in academic prose they are often the result of a writer being so involved in their work that they lose control of their punctuation. This is one of those mistakes that can be spotted after taking a break from writing. It becomes easier to see a fragment when you have a chance to get out of your own head (so you don't unconsciously complete the sentence as you read because you still have it in mind).

A Case of Mistaken Identity

Misspellings

Never forget to run a quick spell-check, but *do* put in the effort to read your work first. Spell-check won't catch incorrect usage if a word is spelled correctly.

They're/There/Their

They're = conjunction of "They are"
> *They're ready to pick you up now.*
> *They are* ready to pick you up now.

There = refers to location (both concrete and abstract). Think: there is a "here" in "there."
> *They're waiting for you over there* (concrete usage).
> *There is a waiting room for visitors in the back* (abstract).

Their = shows possession (plural)
> *Their car was towed while they waited for the doctor.*

You're/Your

You're = conjunction of "You are"
> *You're in for quite a show.*
> *You are in for quite a show.*

Not sure if you should use your or you're? Replace "you're" with "I'm" and see if the sentence makes sense. If it does, you're set.

Your = shows possession.
> *Don't forget to bring your tickets.*

Still not sure? Replace "your" with "my" and try it out. If "my" does the job, the correct usage is "your."

It's/Its

It's = conjunction of "it is" or "it has"

It's been a long week and *it's* not even Wednesday!

It has been a long week and *it is* not even Wednesday!

Its = Neutral possessive (for instance, when referring to an abstract or inanimate object as the possessor)

The party lost its appeal as the night wore on.

The appeal belongs to the party, so the correct usage is "its."

Learn from Others

For some writers, thorough self-editing and revision will result in a polished final draft, ready to be shared or submitted for publication. For the rest of us, there is peer review and feedback. Creative writers call this process finding a critique partner and beta readers. These are readers you know and trust to provide critical feedback that offers support and insight to improve your writing. Generally, these are individuals who know your subject or purpose, but a couple of non-expert readers can also provide critical feedback, particularly on your style and ability to communicate with those who are unfamiliar with your topic.

As a writer, I gain valuable insight from my readers. Students often dismiss the idea of peer review, finding it unhelpful or a waste of time. The problem lies in writers not being prepared for an effective peer review session. Just as you plan your draft, so should you plan for peer review and critique. Don't assume your readers will provide helpful feedback if you don't offer them some insight on the kind of feedback you want to receive. Consider your weaknesses and give your readers a list that they can refer to when reviewing your work. If you feel that your arguments are solid but your paragraphs aren't flowing, ask you readers to focus on this element of your writing. Whether you are interested in receiving feedback on voice, style, or basic grammar, providing your readers with a critique "wishlist" will make their task easier and result in better feedback.

In turn, take the time to grant the same attention to your fellow reader's work; not only will it serve to establish good rapport between you and your critique partner, reading another's writing will help you take note of your own stylistic choices and quirks. I, for one, am overly fond of misplaced modifiers, but it wasn't until I started to give and receive feedback that I noticed my habit of dropping misplaced modifiers throughout my writing. To put it bluntly, reading bad writing is one of the best ways to learn to appreciate good writing. It's the perfect what-not-to-do guide. Reading partners can help you determine where you aren't meeting your reader's needs by identifying passages where you leave your reader floundering for information, or where you alienate them through the use of jargon. A good, critical reader can show you where you need to reevaluate your style and work on your weaknesses. Call this your writing reality check: all those brilliant, idea-generating writing sessions boil down to whether your writing works for your reader. Without a reader in mind, you might as well keep a private journal.

When working with a critique partner, give as good as you get. Telling writers they did a "good job" may do a lot for their ego, but does little for their editing process. Ask for mindful, meaningful feedback, and provide it in return. Quality feedback guides the writer in the right direction by highlighting arguments that are flawed, statements that read awkwardly, and sections where the reader needs more information to understand their reasoning. Quality feedback does not put the writer down or discourage them; it encourages them to take their writing to the next stage.

A final word on working with writing partners and peer editors: you are the ultimate decision-maker when it comes to your writing choices. A review partner can make suggestions and provide critical feedback, but you do not have to apply every change or suggestion if it doesn't fit your goal and vision. Consider their feedback and adapt it to fit your needs. The stronger the relationship with your critique partner, the more likely you are to anticipate each other's needs. A compatible critique partner can help you improve the quality of your work without forcing your writing to fit their own style, or drowning out your voice. You might find that the partner you selected can't give you the level of feedback you need; in such cases, it's fine to thank them for their effort and select a different reader. Finding a compatible writing partner is also a learning process.

Getting to the Final Draft

You've written, edited, and critiqued your way through several drafts; it's over right? Think again. Before you call your draft complete, go back and rewrite your opening; this might be your introduction or the opening line to a sermon, whatever form your writing takes, you may find that your opening statement or section no longer works as well as it did when you first wrote it. When you first write your introduction, you're still becoming accustomed to your subject; you haven't achieved your rhythm yet. When you read through your work, you will find that your writing flows much more easily the further you delve into your writing, revealing your growing expertise and understanding of your subject. You will have even greater control of your writing after several edits, so much so that you may become sick of the subject altogether. Now is the time to rewrite your opening and use that increased awareness to hook your readers with a strong, graceful introduction that will make them want to continue reading or listening to your ideas.

Now you're ready to call it a day. Run your spellchecker one last time, perform a quick line-edit if you're so inclined, check your sources and citations, save, print, and publish.

REVISING AND REWRITING IN TEN EASY STEPS

1. Let your work rest between drafts.

2. Read it all in one sitting (if possible), and start with global revisions. Mark up your page. Look for: redundancies, irrelevant statements, weak arguments, lack of logic, poor flow, filler, etc.

3. Save a separate file as a designated idea dump for those pieces that don't fit. Refer to this file while editing to see if anything is worth keeping in the text.

4. Transcribe your changes and save your draft under a new filename.

5. Read again with an eye towards sentence-level revisions.

   a. Focus on meaning and flow, avoid becoming bogged down by word choice unless variety becomes an issue.

   b. Slash unnecessary words, trim padding, eliminate rambling statements, and watch out for redundant phrases.

   c. And, yes, watch out for your grammar and usage.

6. If in doubt, read your work aloud.

7. Find a writing partner or group to get feedback, and learn when and how to apply criticism.

8. Develop a post-outline if it feels out of order.

9. Consider rewriting your introduction.

10. Spell-check, make any final changes, save, and sigh in relief.

SOME QUESTIONS TO CONSIDER
BETWEEN DRAFTS

1. What was the hardest part of writing?
2. What are my weaknesses as a writer?
3. How can I add more of myself into the next draft?
4. Am I writing with an audience in mind?
5. What is my intention in revising for the next draft?

An Epistle to Authors in Training

Dear Sisters and Brothers,

Thank you for writing theology. Keep faith. Remember, as Kathleen Norris observes, "conversion is a process; it is not a goal, not a product we consume."[1] Your words foster an important part of this conversion for millions of readers, myself included, around the globe. Your words touch us, they move us, they transform us, and they equip us for another day.

We need you to make sense of ourselves and our faith in this bewildering world. We have questions, and when we see that you share the same questions you bring us comfort. You refresh, you renew, and you re-interpret the themes and meanings of our stories of the faith. Your work is vital but also very difficult. Capturing the insights of the Christian faith requires super-human insights. Theologian Thomas Merton explains,

> No writing on the solitary, meditative dimensions of life can say anything that has not already been said better by the wind in the pine trees. These pages seek nothing more than to echo the silence and peace that is "heard" when the rain wanders freely among the hills and forests.[2]

If a great writer like Thomas Merton didn't believe he could capture these dimensions, what hope do we mere mortals have? Luckily for us, most readers don't pay attention to the echoes of silence, so we have an opening and a reason.

As theological writers, we need to work in *kairos* time not chronological time, "kairos time—the right moment, the unplanned insight, the conversation that takes off when participants 'lose track of time.'"[3] This

---

1. Norris, *Amazing Grace*, 42.
2. Merton, *Echoing Silence*, 55.
3. Cameron et al., *Talking about God in Practice*, 66.

doesn't always fit with publishers' schedules and deadlines, or the needs of our checking accounts, but forced writing always sounds false to readers. We need to master bending without breaking.

Theologian Richard Lischer points out "the average American is subjected to approximately six thousand messages per day. Why should one of them called 'gospel' stand out? What is one little message among so many?"[4] I believe that compelling readers will become more and more difficult. But as the challenge grows so does the opportunity. I don't know what the answer will be. A slow theology movement growing out of the slow church movement? A theology of decline? Liquid theologies? Theologies of renewal? But I do believe that no theological system is too big to fail.

As theological writers, we need to remember what Merton wrote: "a bad book about the love of God remains a bad book."[5] The call to write engaged, compelling, and beautiful theological prose only becomes more important as our little messages stand among the myriad messages bombarding readers every day. As writers we must never lose touch with our God, our communities of faith, our sisters and brothers, and our desire to write. Be creative, be courageous, and be the writer you are called to be.

We must inspire and we must push. We will walk into our words. In light of the many unfixable events of life,[6] of the deep places we enter, we can pray that God will empower our imaginations to leap. We can always become better writers of engaged, compelling, and beautiful theology.

Remember: *just keep your feet on the ground.*

4. Lischer, *The End of Words*, 13.

5. Merton, *Echoing Silence*, 102.

6. Epperly, *Process Theology*, 3.

Jonathan's Favorite Novels for Writing

Byatt, A. S. *Possession: A Romance*. New York: Random House, 1990.

Calvino, Italo. *If on a Winter's Night a Traveler*. New York: Harcourt Brace, 1981.

Chandra, Vikram. *Red Earth and Pouring Rain: A Novel*. Boston: Little and Brown, 1995.

Eco, Umberto. *Foucault's Pendulum*. San Diego: Harcourt Brace, 1989.

Fforde, Jasper. *The Eyre Affair: A Novel*. New York: Penguin, 2003.

Heaney, Seamus. *Beowulf: A New Verse Translation*. New York: Farrar, Straus, and Giroux, 2000.

Homer, and E. V. Rieu. *The Illiad of Homer*. Harmonsworth, UK: Penguin Classics, 1957.

Lewis, C. S. *The Lion, the Witch, and the Wardrobe*. New York: HarperCollins, 1994.

Martin, George R. R. *Game of Thrones*. New York: Bantam, 1996.

Michener, James A. *Centennial*. New York: Random House, 1974.

Moore, Christopher. *Lamb: The Gospel according to Biff, Christ's Childhood Pal*. New York: Perennial, 2003.

Niffenegger, Audrey. *The Time Traveler's Wife: A Novel*. San Francisco: MacAdam, 2003.

Robbins, Tom. *Even Cowgirls Get the Blues*. New York: Bantam, 1990.

Rushdie, Salman. *Midnight's Children*. New York: Knopf, 1981.

Tolkien, J. R. R. *The Hobbit, or, There and Back Again*. Boston: Houghton Mifflin, 1966.

Gricel's Favorite Novels for Writing

For a way with words, twists, and turns:

McEwan, Ian. *Atonement: A Novel*. New York:Doubleday, 2002.
Waters, Sarah. *Fingersmith*. New York: Riverhead, 2002.

For humor and turns of phrase:

Carriger, Gail. *Soulless*. New York: Orbit, 2009. (Read the whole *Parasol Protectorate* series.)
Jones, Diana Wynne. *Howl's Moving Castle*. New York: Greenwillow, 1986.

For the sense of time and weight of writing:

Gabaldon, Diana. *Outlander*. New York: Delacorte, 1991.
Martin, George R. R. *Game of Thrones*. New York: Bantam, 1996. (Read the whole series.)

For introspection and the power of words to save us:

Austen, Jane. *Persuasion*. London: Penguin, 1985.
Smith, Dodie. *I Capture the Castle*. Boston: Little and Brown, 1948.

Jonathan's Favorite Books on Writing

Clark, Roy Peter. *Writing Tools: 50 Essential Strategies for Every Writer.* New York: Little and Brown, 2006.

Goldberg, Natalie. *Thunder and Lighting: Cracking Open the Writer's Craft.* New York: Bantam, 2000.

Hale, Constance. *Sin and Syntax: How to Craft Wicked Good Prose.* New York: Three Rivers, 2013.

———. *Vex, Hex, Smash, Smooch: Let Verbs Power Your Writing.* New York: Norton, 2012.

Jacks, G. Robert. *Just Say the Word! Writing for the Ear.* Grand Rapids: Eerdmans, 1996.

King, Stephen. *On Writing: A Memoir of the Craft.* New York: Pocket, 2002.

Lamott, Anne. *Bird by Bird: Some Instruction on Writing and Life.* New York: Anchor, 1995.

Lanham, Richard. *Revising Prose.* 5th Edition. New York: Pearson, 2007.

Leax, John. *Grace is Where I Live: The Landscape of Faith & Writing.* La Porte, IN: WordFarm, 2004.

Merton, Thomas. *Echoing Silence: Thomas Merton on the Vocation of Writing.* Edited by Robert Inchausti. Boston: New Seeds, 2007.

Plotnik, Arthur. *Spunk & Bit: A Writer's Guide to Bold, Contemporary Style.* New York: Random House, 2007.

Sword, Helen. *Stylish Academic Writing.* Cambridge, MA: Harvard University Press, 2012.

Zinsser, William. *On Writing Well.* 30th anniversary edition. New York: Collins, 2006.

Gricel's Favorite Books on Writing

Cook, Claire Kehrwald. *Line by Line: How to Edit Your Own Writing*. Boston: Houghton Mifflin, 1985.

The Modern Language Association's guide to self-editing, this book is aimed towards more experienced writers but offers excellent advice on how to focus on the task of self-editing and revision.

Frank, Steven. *The Pen Commandments: A Guide for the Beginning Writer*. New York: Pantheon, 2003.

This guide is aimed at young writers but is a great resource for writers of all ages. Examples and instructions are presented in a humorous style that makes the tedious task of learning grammar that much more enjoyable.

Fowler, Alastair. *How to Write*. New York: Oxford University Press, 2006.

A short guide that covers all aspects of writing and provides plenty of examples to guide beginning and experienced writers interested in improving their style and usage.

Levine, Becky. *The Writing & Critique Group Survival Guide: How to Give and Receive Feedback, Self-Edit, and Make Revisions*. Cincinnati: Writer's Digest, 2010.

While Levine's book is aimed towards creative writers, there are valuable lessons to be learned for writers of all styles and genres. With individual sections on writing fiction, nonfiction, memoir, and providing criticism in general, the book has advice for all writers interested in learning how to inject imagination into their work, and give and receive effective feedback.

Palmer, Richard. *Write in Style: A Guide to Good English*. 2nd edition. New York: Routledge, 2002.

Palmer's guide provides an overview of the basics of good writing, as well as advice on how to write in an academic context and produce different types of writing (essays, reviews, reports, etc.).

Jonathan's Favorite Books for Theological Methodology

Bevans, Stephen B. *Models of Contextual Theology*. Maryknoll, NY: Orbis, 2002.

Browning, Don S. *A Fundamental Practical Theology: Descriptive and Strategic Proposals*. Minneapolis: Fortress, 1991

Cameron, Helen et al. *Talking about God in Practice*. London: SCM, 2010.

Cameron, Helen, John Reader, and Victoria Slater. *Theological Reflection for Human Flourishing: Pastoral Practice and Public Theology*. London: SCM, 2012.

Cochrane, James. *Circles of Dignity*. Minneapolis: Fortress, 1999.

Cone, James H. *God of the Oppressed*. New York: Seabury, 1975.

———. *A Black Theology of Liberation*. Twentieth anniversary edition. Maryknoll, NY: Orbis, 1990.

De La Torre, Miguel. *Doing Christian Ethics from the Margins*. Maryknoll, NY: Orbis, 2004.

Epperly, Bruce Gordon. *Process Theology: A Guide for the Perplexed*. London: T. & T. Clark, 2011.

Green, Laurie. *Let's Do Theology: Resources for Contextual Theology*. New York: Mowbray, 2009.

Kinast, Robert L. *Let Ministry Teach: A Guide to Theological Reflection*. Collegeville, MN: Liturgical, 1996.

Kwok, Pui-lan. *Postcolonial Imagination and Feminist Theology*. Louisville: Westminster John Knox, 2005.

Lartey, Emmanuel. *Pastoral Theology in an Intercultural World*. Cleveland: Pilgrim, 2006.

Osmer, Richard. *Practical Theology: An Introduction*. Grand Rapids: Eerdmans, 2008.

Sölle, Dorothee, and Shirley Cloyes. *To Work and to Love: A Theology of Creation*. Philadelphia: Fortress, 1984.

Song, Choan-Seng. *The Tears of Lady Meng: A Parable of People's Political Theology*. Geneva: World Council of Churches, 1981.

Stone, Howard, and James Duke. *How to Think Theologically*. 3rd ed. Minneapolis: Fortress, 2013.

Swinton, John, and Harriet Mowat. *Practical Theology and Qualitative Research*. London: SCM, 2006.

Taylor, Barbara Brown. *An Altar in the World: A Geography of Faith*. New York: HarperOne, 2009.

Thistlethwaite, Susan Brooks, and Mary Potter Engel. *Lift Every Voice: Constructing Christian Theologies from the Underside.* Maryknoll, NY: Orbis, 1998.

Thompson, Judith, Stephen Pattison, and Ross Thompson. *SCM Studyguide to Theological Reflection.* London: SCM, 2008.

Vanhoozer, Kevin J., Charles A. Anderson, and Michael J. Sleasman. *Everyday Theology: How to Read Cultural Texts and Interpret Trends.* Grand Rapids: Baker Academic, 2007.

Veling, Terry. *Practical Theology: As Earth as it is in Heaven.* Maryknoll, NY: Orbis, 2005.

Bibliography

Adams, Charles. "Prayer at the Funeral of Rosa Parks." http://www.c-span.org/video/?c3633865/rev-charles-adams-prayer-funeral-rosa-parks.

Alexie, Sherman. *The Lone Ranger and Tonto Fistfight in Heaven.* New York: HarperPerennial, 1994.

Anzaldúa, Gloria. *Borderlands La Frontera: The New Mestiza.* San Francisco: Aunt Lute, 2007.

Arana, Marie. "Introduction." In *The Writing Life: Writers on How They Think and Work,* edited by Marie Arana, xiii–xviii. New York: Public Affairs, 2003.

Augustine. *On Christian Teaching.* New York: Oxford University Press, 2008.

Bajema, Edith. "The Use of Language in Worship." In *The Complete Library of Christian Worship,* edited by Robert Webber, 793–812. Nashville: Star Song, 1999.

"Barth in Retirement." *Time* 81:22 (May 31, 1963) 60.

Berry, Wendell. *The Long-Legged House.* Washington: Shoemaker and Hoard, 2004.

Bevans, Stephen B. *Models of Contextual Theology.* Maryknoll, NY: Orbis, 2002.

Blue, Debbie. *Consider the Birds: A Provocative Guide to Birds of the Bible.* Nashville: Abingdon, 2013.

Browning, Don S. *A Fundamental Practical Theology: Descriptive and Strategic Proposals.* Minneapolis: Fortress, 1991.

Cameron, Helen et al. *Talking about God in Practice.* London, England: SCM, 2010.

Cameron, Helen, John Reader, and Victoria Slater. *Theological Reflection for Human Flourishing: Pastoral Practice and Public Theology.* London, England: SCM, 2012.

Christenson, Tom. "The Oddest Word: Paradoxes of Theological Discourse." In *The Boundaries of Knowledge in Buddhism, Christianity, and Science,* edited by Paul Numrich, 164–83. Göttingen: Vandenhoeck and Ruprecht, 2008.

Clark, Roy Peter. *Writing Tools: 50 Essential Strategies for Every Writer.* New York: Little, Brown and Company, 2006.

Cochrane, James. *Circles of Dignity.* Minneapolis: Fortress, 1999.

Cone, James H. *A Black Theology of Liberation.* Twentieth anniversary edition. Maryknoll, NY: Orbis, 1990.

———. *God of the Oppressed.* New York: Seabury, 1975.

Congar, Yves. *The Meaning of Tradition.* New York: Hawthorn, 1964.

Cook, Claire Kehrwald. *Line by Line: How to Edit Your Own Writing.* Boston: Houghton Mifflin, 1985.

De La Torre, Miguel. *Doing Christian Ethics from the Margins.* Maryknoll, NY: Orbis, 2004.

BIBLIOGRAPHY

Dillard, Annie. *The Writing Life*. New York: HarperPerennial, 1990.

Dorotheus of Gaza. *Discourses and Sayings*. Kalamazoo, MI: Cistercian, 1977.

Edwards, Judson. *Blissful Affliction: The Ministry and Misery of Writing*. Macon, GA: Smyth and Helwys, 2011.

Epperly, Bruce Gordon. *Process Theology: A Guide for the Perplexed*. London: T. & T. Clark, 2011.

Fickett, Harold. "Gushers and Bleeders: On Getting Started." In *A Syllable of Water: Twenty Writers of Faith Reflect on Their Art*, edited by Emilie Griffin, 3–10. Brewster, MA: Parclete, 2008.

Glancy, Diane. "After the Fire of Writing: On Revision." In *A Syllable of Water: Twenty Writers of Faith Reflect on their Art*, edited by Emilie Griffin, 199–209. Brewster, MA: Parclete, 2008.

Goldberg, Natalie. *Thunder and Lightning: Cracking Open the Writer's Craft*. New York: Bantam, 2000.

———. *Writing Down the Bones: Freeing the Writer Within*. Boston: Shambhala, 2010.

Gordon, Mary. "Getting Here from There: A Writer's Reflection on a Religious Past." In *Going on Faith: Writing as a Spiritual Question*, edited by William Zinsser, 19–42. New York: Marlowe, 1999.

Graham, Elaine. *Transforming Practice: Pastoral Theology in an Age of Uncertainty*. Eugene, OR: Wipf & Stock, 2002.

Gratton, Lynda. *The Shift: The Future of Work is Already Here*. London: Collins, 2011.

Gray, Francine Du Plessix. "The Seduction of the Text." In *The Writing Life: Writers on How They Think and Work*, edited by Marie Arana, 3–10. New York: Public Affairs, 2003.

Green, Laurie. *Let's Do Theology: Resources for Contextual Theology*. New York: Mowbray, 2009.

Green, Thomas. *Darkness in the Marketplace: The Christian at Prayer in the World*. Notre Dame, IN: Ave Maria, 1981.

Groome, Thomas. *Sharing Faith: A Comprehensive Approach to Religious Education and Pastoral Ministry: The Way of Shared Praxis*. San Francisco: HarperSanFrancisco, 1991.

Gutiérrez, Gustavo. *We Drink From Our Own Wells: The Spiritual Journey of a People*. Maryknoll, NY: Orbis, 1984.

Hale, Constance. *Sin and Syntax: How to Craft Wicked Good Prose*. New York: Three Rivers, 2013.

———. *Vex, Hex, Smash, Smooch: Let Verbs Power Your Writing*. New York: Norton, 2012.

Hemingway, Ernest. *Ernest Hemingway on Writing*. Edited by Larry W. Phillips. New York: Scribner, 1984.

Hill, Brennan, Paul Knitter, and William Madges. *Faith, Religion & Theology*. Mystic, CT: Twenty-Third, 1997.

Holmes, Emily. "Introduction: Mending a Broken Lineage." In *Women Writing Theology: Transforming a Tradition of Exclusion*, edited by Emily Holmes and Wendy Farley, 1–10. Waco, TX: Baylor University Press, 2011.

Jacks, G. Robert. *Just Say the Word! Writing for the Ear*. Grand Rapids: Eerdmans, 1996.

Kinast, Robert L. *Let Ministry Teach: A Guide to Theological Reflection*. Collegeville, MN: Liturgical, 1996.

King, Stephen. *On Writing: A Memoir of the Craft*. New York: Pocket, 2002.

Kleon, Austin. *Steal Like an Artist*. New York: Workman, 2012.

Klug, Ron. *How to Keep a Spiritual Journal*. Minneapolis: Fortress, 2002.

Kujawa-Holbrook, Sheryl. "Beyond Diversity: Cultural Competence, White Racism Awareness, and European-American Theology Students." *Teaching Theology and Religion* 5:3 (2002) 141–48.

Kwok, Pui-lan. *Postcolonial Imagination and Feminist Theology*. Louisville: Westminster John Knox, 2005.

Lamott, Anne. *Bird by Bird: Some Instruction on Writing and Life*. New York: Anchor, 1995.

Lanham, Richard. *Revising Prose*. 5th edition. New York: Pearson, 2007.

Lartey, Emmanuel. *Pastoral Theology in an Intercultural World*. Cleveland: Pilgrim, 2006.

Leax, John. *Grace is Where I Live: The Landscape of Faith & Writing*. La Porte, IN: WordFarm, 2004.

———. "With Infinite Purposes: On Writing and Place." In *A Syllable of Water: Twenty Writers of Faith Reflect on their Art*, edited by Emilie Griffin, 11–22. Brewster, MA: Parclete, 2008.

Lehmann-Haupt, Christopher. "Books of the Times: 'Incandescent Splendor' a Change in Perception." *New York Times*, September 12, 1980, C21.

Levine, Hillel. "In Search of Sugihara." In *Going on Faith: Writing as a Spiritual Question*, edited by William Zinsser, 67–81. New York: Marlowe and Company, 1999.

Lischer, Richard. *The End of Words: The Language of Reconciliation in a Culture of Violence*. Grand Rapids: Eerdmans, 2005.

Macy, Gary. "The Iberian Heritage of US Latino/a Theology." In *Futuring our Past: Exploration in the Theology of Tradition*, edited by Orlando Espín and Gary Macy, 43–82, Maryknoll, NY: Orbis, 2006.

McCormack, Joseph. *Brief: Make a Bigger Impact by Saying Less*. Hoboken, NJ: Wiley, 2014.

Merton, Thomas. *Echoing Silence: Thomas Merton on the Vocation of Writing*. Edited by Robert Inchausti. Boston: New Seeds, 2007.

———. *The Sign of Jonas*. New York: Harcourt Brace, 1953.

Metz, Johannes Baptist. *Faith in History and Society: Toward a Practical Fundamental Theology*. New York: Seabury, 1980.

Michener, James. "How to Identify and Nurture Young Writers." In *The Writing Life: Writers on How They Think and Work*, edited by Marie Arana, 25–32. New York: Public Affairs, 2003.

Nelson, G. Lynn. *Writing and Being: Taking Back Our Lives through the Power of Language*. San Diego: LuraMedia, 1994.

Norris, Kathleen. *Amazing Grace: A Vocabulary of Faith*. New York: Riverhead, 1998.

Osmer, Richard. *Practical Theology: An Introduction*. Grand Rapids: Eerdmans, 2008.

Palmer, Richard. *Write in Style: A Guide to Good English*. New York: Routledge, 2002.

Pattison, Stephen, and James Woodward, "A Vision of Pastoral Theology: In Search of Words that Resurrect the Dead." In *Spiritual Dimensions of Pastoral Care: Practical Theology in a Multidisciplinary Context*, edited by David Willows and John Swinton, 36–50. Philadelphia: J. Kingsley, 2000.

Pattison, Stephen. *Seeing Things: Deepening Relations with Visual Artefacts*. London, England: SCM, 2007.

Percy, Martyn. *Engaging with Contemporary Culture: Christianity, Theology, and the Concrete Church*. Burlington, VT: Ashgate, 2005.

Phelan, Virginia. *Praying in Your Own Voice through Writing*. Liguori, MO: Liguori, 1994.

BIBLIOGRAPHY

Plotnik, Arthur. *Spunk & Bit: A Writer's Guide to Bold, Contemporary Style.* New York: Random House, 2007.

Prose, Francine. *Reading like a Writer: A Guide for People who Love Books and for Those Who Want to Write Them.* New York: HarperCollins, 2006.

Sawyer, Joy. *The Art of the Soul.* Nashville: Broadman and Holman, 2000.

Sayings of the Desert Fathers. Translated by Benedicta Ward. Kalamazoo, MI: Cistercian, 1984.

Sharp, Melinda McGarrah. *Misunderstanding Stories: Toward a Postcolonial Pastoral Theology.* Eugene, OR: Pickwick, 2013.

Schaap, James Calvin. "Deeper Subjects: On Writing Creative Nonfiction." In *A Syllable of Water: Twenty Writers of Faith Reflect on their Art,* edited by Emilie Griffin, 83–93. Brewster, MA: Parclete, 2008.

Schein, Edgar. *Humble Inquiry: The Gentle Art of Asking Instead of Telling.* San Francisco, CA: Berrett-Koehler, 2013.

Schreiter, Robert. *Constructing Local Theologies.* Maryknoll, NY: Orbis, 1985.

Shaw, Luci. "The Writer's Notebook: On Journal Keeping." In *A Syllable of Water: Twenty Writers of Faith Reflect on their Art,* edited by Emilie Griffin, 23–35. Brewster, MA: Parclete, 2008.

Silverman, Jonathan, and Dean Rader. *The World is a Text: Writing, Reading, and Thinking about Culture and its Contexts.* 2nd edition. Upper Saddle River, NJ: Pearson, 2006.

Sölle, Dorothee, and Shirley Cloyes. *To Work and to Love: A Theology of Creation.* Philadelphia: Fortress, 1984.

Song, Choan-Seng. *In the Beginning Were Stories, Not Texts: Story Theology.* Cambridge: James Clarke, 2012.

———. *The Tears of Lady Meng: A Parable of People's Political Theology.* Geneva: World Council of Churches, 1981.

———. *Tell Us Our Names: Story Theology from an Asian Perspective.* Eugene, OR: Wipf and Stock, 2005.

Stockton, Sarah. *A Pen and a Path: Writing as a Spiritual Practice.* Harrisburg, PA: Morehouse, 2004.

Stone, Howard, and James Duke. *How to Think Theologically.* Minneapolis: Fortress, 2006.

Strunk, William Jr., and E. B. White. *The Elements of Style.* 4th Edition. Boston: Pearson, 1999.

Sword, Helen. *Stylish Academic Writing.* Cambridge, MA: Harvard University Press, 2012.

Swinton, John, and Harriet Mowat. *Practical Theology and Qualitative Research.* London: SCM, 2006.

Taylor, Barbara Brown. *An Altar in the World: A Geography of Faith.* New York: HarperOne, 2009.

Taylor, Daniel. *Creating a Spiritual Legacy: How to Share Your Stories, Values, and Wisdom.* Grand Rapids: Brazos, 2011.

Thiel, John E. *Imagination & Authority: Theological Authorship in the Modern Tradition.* Minneapolis: Fortress, 1991.

Thistlethwaite, Susan Brooks, and Mary Potter Engel, editors. *Lift Every Voice: Constructing Christian Theologies from the Underside.* Maryknoll, NY: Orbis, 1998.

Tilley, Terrence. *Story Theology.* Wilmington, DE: Michael Glazier, 1985.

Tracy, David. *The Analogical Imagination: Christian Theology and the Culture of Pluralism.* New York: Crossroad, 1981.

Bibliography

Truss, Lynne. *Eats, Shoots and Leaves: The Zero Tolerance Approach to Punctuation*. New York: NY: Gotham, 2003.

Vanhoozer, Kevin J., Charles A. Anderson, and Michael J. Sleasman. *Everyday Theology: How to Read Cultural Texts and Interpret Trends*. Grand Rapids: Baker Academic, 2007.

Veling, Terry. "Listening to 'The Voices of the Pages' and 'Combining the Letters: Spiritual Practices of Reading and Writing." *Religious Education* 102 (2007) 206–22.

———. *Practical Theology: As Earth as it is in Heaven*. Maryknoll, NY: Orbis, 2005.

Warren, M. A. C. "Introduction." In *The Primal Vision: Christian Presence Amid African Religion*, edited by John Taylor, 5–12. Philadelphia: Fortress, 1963.

Williams, Thomas. "Saint Anselm." *The Stanford Encyclopedia of Philosophy*. Edited by Edward N. Zalta. http://plato.stanford.edu /archives/ spr2013/ entries/anselm/.

Willimon, William H. *Reading with Deeper Eyes*. Nashville: Upper Room, 1998.

Wilobee, Sondra. *The Write Stuff: Crafting Sermons that Capture and Convince*. Louisville: Westminister John Knox, 2009.

Zinsser, William. *On Writing Well*. 30th anniversary edition. New York: Collins, 2006.

Name and Subject Index